To Dad,
Happy Christmas
1987,
Love Gillian.

GW00360838

THE ESSENTIAL WEST RIDING

THE ESSENTIAL WEST RIDING

Its character in words and pictures

HERBERT WHONE

With a Foreword by
LORD WILSON OF RIEVAULX

1987
SMITH SETTLE
Otley

First published 1975 by
EP Publishing Ltd.

This new edition published 1987 by
Smith Settle
Ilkley Road
Otley
LS21 3JP

Second impression 1987

I.S.B.N.   Paperback   1   870071 05 0
            Hardback   1   870071 06 9

Also by Herbert Whone

The Simplicity of Playing the Violin *Gollancz* 1972
The Hidden Face of Music *Gollancz* 1974
The Integrated Violinist *Gollancz* 1976
Church Monastery Cathedral *Compton Russell Element* 1977
Nursery Rhymes for Adult Children *Tallis Press* 1985
Fountains Abbey *Smith Settle* 1987

Typesetting Ronset, Darwen, Lancs.
Designed, printed and bound by
SMITH SETTLE
ILKLEY ROAD
OTLEY

CONTENTS

Foreword by Lord Wilson   vii
Author's Note   ix
Foreword by J. B. Priestley to the 1975 edition   x
Introduction   xi

ACKNOWLEDGEMENTS

are gratefully due to the following publishers and authors:

Garnstone Press (*Puppets in Yorkshire* – Walter Wilkinson)

Collins (*Crowthers of Bankdam* – Thomas Armstrong)

William Heinemann Ltd. (*Good Companions* – J. B. Priestley)

Curtis Brown Ltd. (*Four Boon Fellows* – Alfred Brown)

Eyre McIntosh (*The Queen of a Distant Country* – John Braine)

Ernest Benn (*English Folk Lore* – A. R. Wright)

Allan Wingate (*Slow Boat through Pennine Waters* – Frederick Doerflinger)

Lawrence & Wishart Ltd. (*Come all ye Bold Miners* – A. L. Lloyd)

Victor Gollancz Ltd. (*The Rise of Henry Morcar* – Phyllis Bentley)

E. P. Group of Companies (*I Haven't Unpacked* – William Holt)

Advertiser Press (*The History of Huddersfield* – Taylor Dyson)

William Beaumont (poem from *Rhymes in the North Country Humour*)

D. H. Holmes (pamphlet *Mining and Quarrying in the Huddersfield District*)

The Huddersfield Examiner (article on canals – Fred Brown)

The Bradford Antiquary (article on Harden Manor – Clifford Whone)

The Times Newspaper (report on pit explosion 1932)

Major J. Fairfax-Blakeborough (*Humours of Village Life*)

Francis Day and Hunter (lyrics of *Stop and Shop at the Co-op Shop*)

Frank Graham (*It's Odd – it's Yorkshire* – Arthur Gaunt)

Dalesman Publishing Co. (*Industrial Revolution in Yorkshire* – Fred Singleton)

A. E. Green and the Director, The Institute of Dialect and Folk Life Studies, The
University, Leeds (folk songs – *The Weaver's Lament and Leeds Owd Church*)

Messrs. Watmough, Bradford (*The Clock Almanack* and sayings – John Hartley)

The Yorkshire Dialect Society and the authors (poems by Fred Brown, W. J. Halliday; also
The Weaver from *White Rose Garland*)

FOREWORD

Born in Milnsbridge, in Huddersfield, in March 1916, my earliest memory was in Old Byland near Rievaulx on Peace Day 1918 – I'll never forget the brass band playing on that day! My great enthusiasm in Milnsbridge was scouting, since my father was Rover Leader, my sister a Girl Guide and Ranger, and I ultimately managed, within a few days of my eighteenth birthday, to become a King's Scout. Indeed the chapel which we attended had the biggest scout troop in the whole of Yorkshire, and a few miles from the Colne Valley, away from the smoke, we had a permanent camping site between Meltham and Honley and sometimes I would camp, with a friend, near Rievaulx Abbey.

No account of life in the 1920s and early 1930s bears any relation to priorities so strongly as the success of our soccer team, Huddersfield Town. If I remember rightly, we were top of the league's First Division three years in succession, and in two cup finals (unfortunately losing both). More than half a century later, I still carry in my wallet a small photograph of the team of those years. My father was a Works Manager in dyestuffs and chemicals at part of L B Holliday's works down the road from town – who were in constant competition with a firm which was later to become ICI – but when I was sixteen he lost his job. After months of unemployment, he eventually secured work in Cheshire, and my family moved to the Wirral Peninsula, but my loyalties still remained on the other side of the Pennines!

In historical terms, my real connection was not with Huddersfield but with Rievaulx about fifty miles to the north, and where I had camped as a boy. When I was elected Leader of Her Majesty's Opposition in 1963, a year before becoming Prime Minister for the first time, a national newspaper commissioned Garter, King of Arms, the unchallenged expert of heredity, to trace me back in the male line as far as he could. His report showed clearly that my family had lived in Rievaulx, or somewhere in Rydale within three or four miles of Rievaulx, as far back as the 1490s. I also have historical connections with York, as my great-grandfather Wilson was Workhouse Master there, after a successful and humane period as Workhouse Master at Helmsley, workhouses being a great step forward in improving social conditions at that time and for years afterwards. I have always been fascinated by York and its long and varied history not only since, but also long before, my election as an honorary freeman of that great city.

Thirty-five years after my enforced departure from my native county, the newly-created University of Bradford elected me as its Chancellor in 1966, and so for the last eighteen years – until my recent resignation as Chancellor – I have happily gone back time and again to the "County of broad acres and broad vowels". Mr Whone in his book has well recalled the scenes and language of my West Riding childhood. I wish it success – I am sure it will give pleasure to all those who have been born there.

WILSON OF RIEVAULX 1987

AUTHOR'S NOTE ON THIS EDITION

It is now twelve years since The Essential West Riding was first printed. Regrettably, after two re-issues, it remained out of print. The reasons were not connected with the demand, for during that period I received numerous enquiries from West Ridingers at home and around the world. Somehow they had seen a copy and wrote to say the book epitomised the spirit and atmosphere of their birth-place, and where please could they get one for themselves. I am grateful therefore, that Smith Settle have undertaken to re-issue the book in its original form, especially since its presentation has been revised and much improved.

It is true that since 1975, the inevitable bull-dozer of progress has flattened some of the buildings depicted – for example, the back-to-backs in John Street, Crossflatts, lived in by my grandmother, which are now no more: it has also eliminated the cheering naked light of gas-lamps in town and country; and chapels are becoming fewer and fewer. The book came at a time of transition – a painful time when the beautiful gave way to the utilitarian. Still, a great deal of what it portrays remains, and it obviously means a lot to those of my generation, and to the generation of my own children. Even the present younger generation sees the West Riding language and tradition perpetuated in the television series 'The Last of the Summer Wine'. However much the name may recede into the past, the West Riding, as a colourful aspect of our national history, lives on, and the name will come automatically to the lips for years to come. Its rugged landscape and equally rugged people are unique.

I hope this edition of 'The Essential West Riding' continues to give pleasure to those who have had the privilege of being nurtured here, and to others who wonder what the mystique is all about.

HERBERT WHONE,
Harrogate, 1987.

FOREWORD TO THE 1975 EDITION

I have now lived eighty years and I may be said to have spent sixty of them living well away from the West Riding. I have in fact passed more of my time in London than I have in Bradford or anywhere else in the West Riding. Moreover, if we take the bulk of my work in various forms, only a small portion of it is concerned with Yorkshire: I am far from being a regional writer. Yet here I am, introducing a book about the West Riding.

Quite right, too! Those first twenty years left an indelible mark on me. I remain a West Riding man. I feel at home as soon as I get back. (Then why don't I live there? Partly because it is an inconvenient distance from London, and partly too because the winters are harder than they are just outside Stratford-upon-Avon. Again, my wife is not a Yorkshire woman and my children and grandchildren all live in the South.) And indeed – and this will surprise some readers – I have always liked *the look of the West Riding,* and I am thinking now not about the moors and dales but about the towns, which have been able to take a certain dignity, even a touch of beauty, from their blackened stone. However, perhaps I ought to qualify this, if only because too many unsuitable buildings, often looking as if they were dreamt up in Los Angeles, have been recently erected, neither pleasing in themselves nor pleasing as a contrast to old blackened stone. It may be my age and its prejudices, but I certainly prefer the old West Riding to the newer one, which tries to look as if it were somewhere else.

Because of my profession, I concentrate on human nature and character just as some other people concentrate on birds or flowers. And, as an expert, I am sure that West Riding people are largely misunderstood. This is partly due to the local accent, which I still share though not in its broader or more nasal style. Its open vowels and sharply chiselled consonants encourage visitors from the South to imagine that Yorkshire folk are blunter and grimmer than they really are. Moreover, the underlying irony and rather sardonic humour are often missed. Again, just as people elsewhere often pretend to be more sensitive than they really are, West Riding types often pretend to be far less sensitive, and may be artists at heart when they are almost giving a performance as wool buyers. And here I might add that the number of artists, writers, musicians, actors, my native city of Bradford has produced is *astounding.* I have been running into them, generation after generation, for the last sixty years, some of them thousands of miles away. One other point: one would think from what some outsiders write or say that West Riding folk hardly know how to begin enjoying themselves whereas they tend to be enormous enjoyers, better at it, I would say, than most Midlanders or Southerners. I am now almost famous for grumbling and yet enjoying myself, and this makes me a fairly typical West Riding man.

With this subject of enjoyment still in mind, perhaps I may be allowed a tiny grumble against Mr. Whone's otherwise admirable book. Even though the text is varied and the photographs are wonderful, he does tend to support the legend that the West Riding is a grim place with people not largely given to enjoying themselves. In this respect he does not show me *my own* West Riding, that is, not in its entirety but only in certain aspects of it. But once we allow him these aspects, he seems to me to have done a very good job indeed. His wide choice of quotations, some from unusual sources, can hardly be bettered. As for the photographs, I repeat, they are wonderful, and though sombre as most of them are, they began to make me feel homesick. And I hope this book will have the success it well deserves to have, both inside and outside the West Riding.

J. B. Priestley

INTRODUCTION

My ancestors have been Yorkshiremen since their name first appeared as WAGHEN or WAWNE, after a Saxon village near Beverley recorded in the Domesday Book. Later there were migrations Westwards, one of which ended in Thornton in Craven near Skipton where my own particular line is recorded in Parish Registers from the 16th century onwards. Some years ago I knew nothing of who my ancestors had been, but as I unearthed their history a simple pattern emerged: all of them had been weavers and from a study of the time it is safe to assume that this is what they had been long before recorded entries.

There were changes in the family fortune however. Walne's Farm as it was called, near Thornton, where the trade of weaving was carried out had to be abandoned at the end of the 18th century, and like so many other small owners the family was obliged to move closer to the industries of Lancashire – in this case Colne, for work. Then later my great-grandfather fled the terrible privations of the 1830s and '40s due to the decline in the cotton trade, and went to find work in the woollen mills in the Aire valley in Yorkshire. It was here in Micklethwaite near Bingley that my immediate ancestors settled and lived for another hundred and thirty years, and it is from here that my own memories as a child stem; for though we lived in Bingley, my father made two journeys to the Weslyan Reform Chapel at Micklethwaite four miles away almost every Sunday of his life. This then, very broadly is the family story.

It is hard to describe the feelings I experienced as those early registers revealed the pattern of life my ancestors had led – I saw only stark entries of birth, marriage, work and death, and the uncertain crosses that were their signatures. They were a poignant link with the past and I felt gratitude towards those men and women who had lived their anonymous lives before me. I realised, above all, that I was seeing through their eyes – that in my paintings and in the photographs in this book, I was embodying all their experience. I felt the continuity that made me what I am, and in a way I knew it was they, not I, who were doing the work. Even my gift for music could be seen in my father's Sunday School writings.

In my early years then I absorbed the customs, scenery and dialect of the West Riding, and at the age of nineteen left home drawn by the needs of a profession. But at the age of forty, circumstances called for a change and I found myself being pulled back to the scene of my childhood. And as I walked, sketched, and tracked down my family tree, I became fascinated by its unique landscape, the quality of which I had found nowhere else, either in this country or abroad. Nowhere had I seen such variety and spontaneity in both nature and the works of man. Mountains of stone, it seemed, had been heaved up in a superhuman way no less astonishing than the pyramids themselves. Beauty in utility was everywhere around me – beauty in the infinite variety of stiles, walls, wrought iron gates; and beauty in the stone arches of barn and factory and in the design even of the tips of mill chimneys.

Man, it seemed, had defied nature, and everywhere nature had lashed back, defiantly producing a display of unpredictability that the most ingenious artist would have been hard pressed to draw from his imagination. The conflict between man and nature was to be seen in the streams ceaselessly pouring through gaps in walls, in moss-covered roof-tops, in gates leaning and broken from their hinges, in gas-lamps and in the broken pattern of countless paths struggling for survival through fields and over moors. And in this strange landscape there was a feeling of the end of an era. Everywhere progress was encroaching upon its beauty – graveyards were being uprooted, chapels razed to the ground, back-to-backs being eliminated for blocks of flats, and motor-ways being cut through the centre of villages. And now as I write in 1974 the very name West Riding has officially disappeared from use.

This collection of photographs then, taken over a period of seven years, and the writings that accompany them, are one West Ridinger's attempt to record his own land and traditions. They are essentially a recovery of all that has lain buried since childhood, and also as I have said, in the experience of my ancestors. Ben Preston, John Hartley and Bill o'th Hoylus End, only names when I was a child, have become real people and real artists – I feel I know their language as well as if I had lived in their time. Photography itself is also a recovery of the past, for I was taking pictures of the landscape with my father's box camera at the age of fourteen – something in the landscape impressed me even then. The key-note to the photographs in this book is spontaneity. I have found that setting out with the intention of taking pictures has scarcely ever succeeded. An artist must find his own spontaneity when he paints a picture, but a photograph only lives if it has presented itself unexpectedly: then the hand has to react in a moment or the gift is lost. I should also add that in some cases the places in the photographs have drastically changed – the progress we can not escape has taken away a lamp, a chimney or even a whole building. As to the writings accompanying the pictures, I have drawn largely from authors whom I felt has the feel of the West Riding in their blood: I am only sorry that I have had to omit some living dialect poets whose work I admire. When using dialect poems I have referred to the earliest editions, despite the fact of grammatical anomalies, apostrophes, spelling and so on, for though they have been righted in later editions, words have been changed too.

"The Essential West Riding" is then, as the title suggests, not by way of a tourist guide to specific places, though the places are identified for interest in the index. They range over the whole of the West Riding scene, and are not important to the purpose of the book. The aim has been to capture the essence of the area. For this reason I have not shown people in the photographs – to have done so would have localised the book to a few years in time: and for the same reason, though there is a connecting link, I have attempted no exact correspondence between the words and picture. Finally, it will not surprise readers when I say that I dedicate this book reverently to my father, to his father, and his father, and his father before him.

Herbert Whone
Harrogate 1974

SPECIAL ACKNOWLEDGEMENT

To conceive this book was one thing, but to make it real would not have been possible without the co-operation of my friend, photographer Ken Baldwin, ARPS, official photographer of the restoration of York Minster and former winner of the *Financial Times* "Photographer of the Year" award. He has made up for my lack of technical expertise in the darkroom by producing enlargements that surpassed my expectations. How closely we felt on the subject is indicated by the fact that we have not disagreed on the treatment of any of the negatives. In fact I know that his artistry has often enhanced a negative that has not been of the highest quality, and I am very grateful to him for his skill, imagination and time.

H.W.

TO
BRADFORD
4 MILES

TO
HALIFAX
5¼ MILES

However disagreeable or amusing such a description may be to a man who is disposed to regard himself (if he takes the trouble to think about it at all) as the King of the Forest, he has to admit that outside two or three adjacent counties his character is not well understood – indeed, is generally misunderstood – and the "typical" Yorkshireman is looked upon as a man of boorish manners and uncouth speech; a hard bargainer, whether as master or man; intolerant and consequently intolerable; nauseously self-satisfied and pig-headed; as indifferent to the refinements of good society as the animal whose head he is supposed to have borrowed; a worshipper of one idol and one only – Ruskin's "Goddess of Getting-on"; a stage clown, not far removed from a stage villain; with only one virtue grudgingly granted him, that of a measureless and ungrudging hospitality. Not a very attractive portrait.

For much of this misconception, or partial misconception, I admit Yorkshiremen have only themselves to blame. That they are "queer-sticks" none of them would deny. The estimates of outsiders only amuse them; they take pleasure in offering their detractors more evidence with which to weigh the scale of adverse judgement. They profess to approve the Yorkshire maxim – "If tha does owt for nowt, do it for thysen", and quote it with a seriousness that completely cloaks the underlying humour. A hard bargainer your typical Yorkshireman undoubtedly is, and a confirmed believer in the advantages of accumulating "brass"; but the main difference between him and others is probably to be found in his dislike of pretence and cant, in his willingness to admit and even to exaggerate his weaknesses and faults; and there is no reason to suppose that if he is a little cleverer at a bargain than the majority of Englishmen he is any more grasping.

The Yorkshireman has, in fact, many of the qualities of the moors on which, or on whose edges, he dwells. He is often harsh, gnarled, prickly; tenacious of his rights and only roughly picturesque; but he has many characteristics that are admirable and distinctly English: he has a dogged perseverance, great strength of will, sound judgment, ready wit. And withal he has a heart that is very tender.

from *A Yorkshire Suburb*
W. Riley (published 1920)

Hart Street, Great Horton Road, Bradford

We climbed interminably, a purgatorial, bumpy way among the grey houses. It was a northern city, a forest of grey stone. Mills, like fortresses, loomed enormously; innocent suites of offices were enshrined in rugged castles, and the houses were as strong as goals. There were stumpy little streets, rocky retreats, where sturdy, bare-armed women gossiped unashamedly across the road. There was an occasional old grandmother with a shawl over her head, and, rarely, the clatter of clogs on the pavement.

Wesley Methodist Church, Southowram, near Halifax

Would we ever reach this school at the top of the hill. There was no end to this avenue of stone, or of the granite sets. We passed more and more of those high, hilly streets, where the vigorous air must be always moving, nourishing the sturdy heroes who live there. We looked back at the city sinking away into the misty, smoky valley miles below, and emerging again to new heights on the other side. It was tremendous, and I began to understand something of the northern spirit, the mighty determination which, on this impossible site, has reared the city, commencing in the valley and climbing, street by street, the steep towering valley side.

from *Puppets in Yorkshire*
Walter Wilkinson
(published 1931)

3

Outlane, Huddersfield

And if we compare the local names in England with those on the Continent, we shall find that for more than a thousand years England has been distinctively and pre-eminently the land of enclosures. The suffixes which occur most frequently in Anglo-Saxon names denote an enclosure of some kind – something hedged, walled in, or protected. An examination of these names shows us that the love of privacy, and the seclusiveness of character which is so often laid to the charge of Englishmen, prevailed in full force among the races which imposed names upon our English villages. Those universally recurring terminations *ton, ham, worth, stoke, fold, garth, burgh, bury, brough, borrow,* all convey the notion of enclosure or protection.

from *Words and Places*
Isaac Taylor (published 1911)

East Morton from Micklethwaite, near Bingley

Names and towns in Yorkshire derived from the Norse or Scandinavian language and ending in *by,* meaning a village or town

Quarmby (W.R. Huddersfield district)	— The quern, or millstone town, from quarnarstein.
Sowerby (W.R. Halifax district)	— Sowertown, from sai, to sow corn.

with Norse terminations *thorpe* meaning landed estate or field

Austhorpe (W.R. Hunslet district)	— the East thorpe
Thorpe (W.R. Wakefield district)	

ending in *holme* meaning an island or meadow

Hipperholme (W.R. Halifax district)	— the wild boar's meadow
Holmfirth (W.R. Huddersfield district)	— the meadow enclosure. Firth is from the British word Frith, an enclosure.

ending in *thwaite* – meaning a clearing in a forest

Micklethwaite (W.R. Keighley district)	— the great clearing
Slaithwaite (W.R. Huddersfield district)	— the sloe-tree clearing from sla, a sloe-tree.

ending or beginning in *thorn* – meaning a thorn hedge or enclosure

Bagthorne (Keighley district)	— the beach-tree enclosure, from bag, beech-tree.

ending in *royd* (riodr) which means a clearing

Mytholmroyd	— the girl's meadow clearing, from mey, a girl, holm, a meadow and riodr, a clearing.

from *Yorkshire Past and Present*
Thomas Baines (published 1871)

Pole Moor looking towards Slaithwaite

Cobden Street, Sowerby Bridge

He walked to the window, the outside sill of which was mottled with the black and white of melting snow. His dark eyes were on the high ground to the far side of the valley, where the white of the skyline was still pure against the leaden sky. As his glance fell so did the perfection of that purity fade as it neared grey industry and the lower limits where the Ram, not over-swollen yet, wound darkly between borders whose colour ranged between ivory and puddled brown. On the wind-stung slopes of Garthedge and Cowgill Summit, the drifts might be anything up to twice the height of a Ramsfield man, but in the valley it was seldom that snow, in its pristine form, lingered very long. The roofs in the town were already showing irregular margins of wet-blackened grey stone tiles; the branches of the Moorheaton trees, beginning to drip, carried an amorphous powder which had died before it had the chance to scintillate; and the ever-optimistic children of the district would be lucky to find an incline on which the steel runners of their sledges did not throw to both sides a gritty and watery cascade.

from *The Crowthers of Bankdam*
Thomas Armstrong (published 1940)

Scammonden area, Huddersfield

Hillhouse, Huddersfield

The tram had ground its way to the Black Swan Inn (known locally as "t'Mucky Duck"), and this was his stop. He walked, rather slowly and heavily the few hundred yards that brought him to Ogden Street.

Nobody could consider Ogden Street very attractive; it was very long and very drab, and contained two rows of singularly ugly black little houses; yet Ogden Street had its boasts, and its residents could claim to have both feet on the social ladder. You could, in fact, have a "come-down" from Ogden Street, and there were some people who even saw it as a symbol of a prosperity long vanished. To begin with, it was a respectable street, not one of those in which you heard sudden screams in the night or the sound of police whistles. Then too, it was entirely composed of proper houses, all with doors opening onto the street; and in this respect it was unlike its neighbours at the back, Velvet Street and Merino Street, which had nothing but "passage" or "back-to-back" houses, the product of an ingenious architectural scheme that crammed four dwelling-places into the space of two and enabled some past citizens to drive a carriage-and-pair and take their wives and daughters to the Paris Exhibition in 1867.

Queensbury

"Na Jess!" said the acquaintance, taking an imitation calabash pipe out of his mouth and then winking mysteriously.

"Na Jim!" returned Mr. Oakroyd. This "Na", which must once have been "Now", is the recognised salutation in Bruddersford, and the fact that it sounds more like a word of caution than a word of greeting is by no means surprising. You have to be careful in Bruddersford.

two excerpts from *The Good Companions*
J. B. Priestley (published 1929)

11

Slaithwaite viaduct

Canal at Luddenden Foot

Scammonden area, Huddersfield

In the Huddersfield district much of the land enclosure was by means of dry stone walls, and during the nineteenth century, especially up to 1860, much of the surrounding area was walled . . . The smallholders of land, who could not afford the cost of enclosure and also the commoner who could no longer keep his sheep on the moor were driven to other occupations and turned either to industry, mining, quarrying or walling. In our district the lot of the agricultural labourer was not as difficult as in the south of England, where rioting took place against Land Enclosure, since the aforesaid industries provided some occupation.

Hardcastle Crags, Hebden Bridge

Much of the walling was done by "gangs" – i.e., a man would contract with the local landowner to provide labour for the walling, and teams of men, women and children would hew the rock from the quarries and cart it to the walling site where the more skilled men constructed the walls. The skill of these men is manifested in the fact that these walls are still standing despite a century and a half of buffeting by wind and rain, in some of the wildest parts of the Pennines.

from *Mining and Quarrying in the*
Huddersfield District
D. H. Holmes (pamphlet in Tolson
Memorial Museum)

15

Near Brontë Falls, Haworth

Pole Moor, near Huddersfield

The night is darkening around me,
The wild wind coldly blows;
But a tyrant spell has bound me,
And I cannot, cannot go.

Clouds beyond clouds above me,
Wastes beyond wastes below,
But nothing drear can move me:
I will not, cannot go.

The giant trees are bending
Their bare boughs weighed with snow;
The storm is fast descending,
And yet I cannot go.

By *Emily Brontë* (1837) when 18 years
of age

Owd Moxy

Owd Moxy rowt hard for his morsel
  o' bread,
An' ta keep up his courage he'd sing,
Thau Time wi' his scythe had maun
  t'crop on his eead,
An' then pufft it away wi' his wing.

Reyt slavish his labour an' little his
  wage,
His path tuv his grave wor bud rough,
Poor livin' an' 'ardships, a deal moar
  nur age,
Hed swealed dahn his cannal to
  t'snuff.

One cow'd winter morn, as he crept
  aht o' bed,
T'owd waller felt dizzy an' soar:–
"Come, frame us some breykfast, Owd
  Duckfooit," he said,
"An' ah'll finish yond fence up at
  t'moor;

"Al tew like a brick wi' my hammer an'
  mawl,
An' ah'll bring hoam my honey to
  t'hive,
An' ah'll pay t'bit o' rent an' wer shop-
  score an' all,
An' ah'll dee aht o' debt if ah live."

Soa Peg made his pobs an' then
    futtered abaht,
An' temm'd him his tea into t'can,
Then teed up some bacon an' bread
    in a claht,
Fur dearly shoo liked her owd man.

Then Moxy set aht on his wearisome
    way,
Wadin' bravely thru t'snaw broth i'
    t'dark;
It's a pity when fellahs at's wakely an'
    grey
Hes ta walk for a mile to ther wark.

Bud summat that mornin' made Moxy
    turn back,
Thau he 'ardly knew what it could
    meean,
Soa cudlin Owd Peggy he gave her a
    smack,
An' then started for t'common ageean.

All t'day a wild hurrikin wuther'd thru
    t'glen,
An' then rusht like a fiend up to
    'heeath;
An' as Peggy sat knitting' shoo sed tuv
    hersen
"Aw dear! he'll be starruv'd to
    t'deeath."

An' shoo felt all day as shoo'd ne'er
    felt afoar,
An' shoo dreaded yit hungar'd for
    neet;
When harknin' an tremlin' shoo eeard
    abaht t'doar
A mutterin' an' shufflin' o' feet.

Five minits at after, Owd Peg, on her
    knees,
Wor kussin' a foreead like stoan;
An' to t'men at stood by her wi' tears i'
    ther ees,
Shoo sed, "Goa, lads, an' leave ma
    aloan."

When they streytened his body, all
    ready for t'kist,
It wor seen at he'd thowt of his plan,
For t'shop-score an t'rent wor safe
    lockt in his fist,
Soa he deed aht o' debt, like a man.

from *Ben Preston, his collected poems*
    by J. E. Preston 1872

Booth Bank, Slaithwaite

19

Belfry, East Marton Church, near Skipton

Close to whear he lived ther wor a chap 'at kept a sausage shop, an' he wor takken sick an' deed, an' his widder sent for Tommy to come an' shave him befoor he wor burrid, an' he did it i' sich a nice an' considerate way, an' tawked soa solemn, an' pooled sich a long face, 'at he gate invited to th' funeral, an wor axed to be one o' th'bearers, an' as he nobbut stood abaat four feet in his booits, he consented at once, for as t'other five chaps all stood abaat six feet, he knew he wouldn't have mich to carry.

Holywell Green, near Elland

When th'funeral wor nicely ovver, an' they gate back to th'haase, they were all invited to stop an' have a bit o' summat to ait, an' as sausage wor th'handiest o' owt to cook shoo axed 'em if they'd have some. Nubdy'd owt to say ageean it, but Tommy didn't seem satisfied, an when th'widder saw it shoo sed, "may be, Tommy, sausage doesn't agree wi' you – is their owt else yo'd like."

"Well," he sed, "aw've nowt ageean sausage, but aw think at black pudding wod be moor appropriate for a burrin."

from *Yorkshire Puddin'*
John Hartley (published 1877)
from the chapter "Why Tommy isn't a Deacon"

A friend well acquainted with the place when Charlotte Brontë was at school, has described some events which occurred then among them:—

"A scene, which took place at the Lower Chapel at Heckmondwike, will give you some idea of the people at that time. When a newly-married couple made their appearance at chapel, it was the custom to sing the Wedding Anthem, just after the last prayer, and as the congregation was quitting the chapel. The band of singers who performed this ceremony expected to have money given to them, and often passed the following night in drinking; at least, so said the minister of the place; and he determined to put an end to this custom. In this he was supported by many members of the chapel and congregation; but so strong was the democratic element, that he met with the most violent opposition, and was often insulted when he went into the street. A bride was expected to make her first appearance, and the minister told the singers not to perform the anthem. On their declaring they would, he had the large pew which they usually occupied locked; they broke it open: from the pulpit he told the congregation that, instead of their singing a hymn, would read a chapter; hardly had he uttered the first word, before up rose the singers, headed by a tall fierce-looking weaver, who gave out a hymn, and all sang it at the very top of their voices, aided by those of their friends who were in the chapel. Those who disapproved of the conduct of the singers and sided with the minister, remained seated till the hymn was finished. Then he gave out the chapter again, read it and preached. He was just about to conclude with prayer, when up started the singers and screamed forth another hymn."

from *Life of Charlotte Brontë*
Mrs Gaskell (published 1880)

Graveyard, Bingley Parish Church

Sowerby village

United Methodist Chapel, Luddenden Foot

Disused Chapel at Lockwood, Huddersfield

May 29th 1743

. . . a spark has now fallen in this place (Leeds) also, and it will kindle a great flame. I met the infant society, about fifty in number, most of them justified, and exhorted them to walk circumspectly. At seven o'clock I stood before Mr. Shent's door, and cried to thousands, "Ho, every one that thirsteth, come ye to the waters". The word took place. They gave diligent heed to it, and seemed a people prepared for the Lord.

June 9th 1757

I rode over the mountains to Huddersfield. A wilder people I never saw in England: the men, women and children filled the streets as we rode along, and appeared just ready to devour us. They were, however tolerably quiet whilst I preached; only a few pieces of dirt were thrown; and the bellman came in the middle of the sermon, but was stopped by a gentleman of this town. I had almost done when they began to ring the bells; so that it did us no small disservice. How intolerable a thing is the Gospel of Christ to them who are resolved to serve the Devil!

from *The Diaries of John Wesley*

St. Andrew's United Reformed Church, Westgate, Bradford

27

Methodist Church, Mount Tabor, near Halifax

Dish Cloth

I have said that some of Abe's similies were not very elegant, and when the following is related, my readers will agree with me; but they were well understood by the people among whom they were uttered. Speaking one day of the pardoning mercy of God, and showing that he does not grudgingly forgive the penitent sinner, Abe said:

"You women folk know how to wash a pie dish, I reckon? you'll tak' th'dish and put it into th'hot water, and then tak' dish cloth and rub it raand and raand, inside and aatside, till it's clean, and then you'll wipe it wi' a clean towel, and mak' it look just loike a bron new dish; and that's haa th'Lord does wi' a poor sinner; he gies him a plunge into the gospel fountain, washes all his sins away, and brings him aat a bron new man."

An old woman sitting there caught the figure in a moment and responded energetically, "Maa th'Lord tak" dish cloth and wipe some aat here t'noight!"

"Amen", exclaimed "the Bishop".

> from *Little Abe or The Bishop of Berry Brow*
> (Abraham Lockwood)
> J. Jewell (a Methodist publication of 1880)

Ther wor another owd "local" at wor mich sowt after at anniversaries, an' he us'td to brag hah mich he'd getten at collections. One Sunday he wor preyching at Low Moor Weslyans, an' a lot o'fowk thru rahnd abaht cam' to hear him. T'chappil wor ommost crammed as he wor going' up t'pulpit steps, but seein' a crahd blockin' up t'doorway, he sings aht –"Nah then, ye Low Moorers, mak' way for t'Wibsa chaps, an' let t'hauf-crahners cum forrad!"

> from *Yorkshire Speyks*
> William Cudworth (published 1906)
> from the chapter "Local Preychers"

29

Graveyard, Methodist Church, Mount Tabor, near Halifax

"But as for fowk not likin poitri," ah sez, "ah doant call it a case o' better an' wahr, misen, ah call it a matter o' taste. Ah hoap an' trust," ah sez, "an' soa duz Flather, 'at a man can goa to Heaven if he lives a gooid life baht bein' partic'lar fond o' poitri, barrin' it's a gooid owd hymn or t'like o' that. Ah'm middlin fond ont' missen when it's reyt up t'mark, but it's a bit like Yorksher puddin', is poitri," ah sez. "There's nowt nicer when it is nice, wi' a sup o' gooid beef gravy – an' when ah sez gravy ah mean gravy, not weshin' up wotter – but ther's plenty 'at can't mak a Yorkshire puddin' fit to eyt. They'll gi'e tha a gurt dollop o' clammy soggy stuff 'at looks an' tastes as mich like putty as owt, an' wi' gurt lumps o' raw flahr i't' middle; or happen it'll be same as a buffalo hide wi' black blisters all ower it. 'an it's t'same wi poitri."

from an *Abe Clegg talk*
F. J. Newbolt
first published 1918-22 in the
Yorkshire Observer

Graveyard, Ovenden Parish Church, near Halifax

Slaithwaite

Plumpton Road, Wakefield

Queer Times Pudding

1 cupful of bread crumbs, 1 cupful of flour, 1 cupful of currants, 2 ozs. suet, pinch of salt, 1 cupful sugar, 2 teaspoonfulls baking powder. Mix all together with a little milk and steam for 2 hours.

Right Bread for War Prisoners
(which will keep for a month)

2 lbs. risen dough, 2 ozs. lard, 1 teaspoonful castor sugar. Knead the lard and sugar into the dough and bake in a spare baking tin to a nice brown. N.B. Be sure not to pack up the bread until at least 24 hours old.

from *A Yorkshire Cookery Book*
(Wakefield 1916)

33

"Aw shud think so, i'deed," cried my mother; "my own sister. If yo' can't look to yo'r own i' th'time o'need, what's relations for aw shud like to know. Onybody'll stan' yo'r friend when yo'r i' no need o'friends. It's trouble tries folk. Nah, thee drink this cup o'tea, Matty, an' nivver heed drawin' to th'table. Sit wheer th'art an' keep thi feet on th'fender. An' see yo', there's a drop o'rum i' th'tea, tho' aw donnut hold wi' it as a reg'lar thing, for wilful waste ma'es woful want, but it'll warm thee an' hearten thi up. Tha' looks as if tha' hadn't a drop o'blood in thi body poor thing."

"I cannot tell wher' yo'r wits are these days, said 'Siah impatiently. "Theer tha' sits bi th'fireside, countin' th'cowks an' glowering into th'ass-hoil as if that 'ud do thi ony good. Tha' should stir abaht, man, an' hear what's afoot. There's more inspiration, as th'parson calls it, to be fun at th'Black Bull i' hauf an hour nor i' a week o' sulkin' at whom bi thissen."

two excerpts from Ben O'Bills (The Luddite)
D. F. E. Sykes (published 1896)

Bracken Street, Springbank, Keighley

Scarr Head Road, Sowerby Bridge

It was a bitter February night in the Great Snow of 1947. The barber
had closed his shop, and with an elderly lady, had battled his way through
the gale from the bus terminus at Siddal to some remote cottage beyond. He
had agreed to "come and shave Joe". Joe was the lady's husband. As she
inserted a large key into the lock, she enquired "An ar much do yo' charge for
shavin' like?" The barber, chilled and blue of face said "Oh, a tanner for an
old customer like Joe. We've missed 'im yo' kno'. Esn't 'e been sa weel?"
"No," said the lady, " 'e asn't. An' e' deed this mornin'." "Oh well, that's
diff'rent," countered the barber – "It's allus awf-a-crahn for shavin' a stiff-
un." "Awf-a-crahn!" cried the lady, aghast – "Well, nah then, aw doant think
aw'll bother; it isn't as if 'e were gooin' onnywheer partickler."

from *Story of the Town that Bred Us (Halifax)*
compiled by J. J. Mulroy (published 1948)

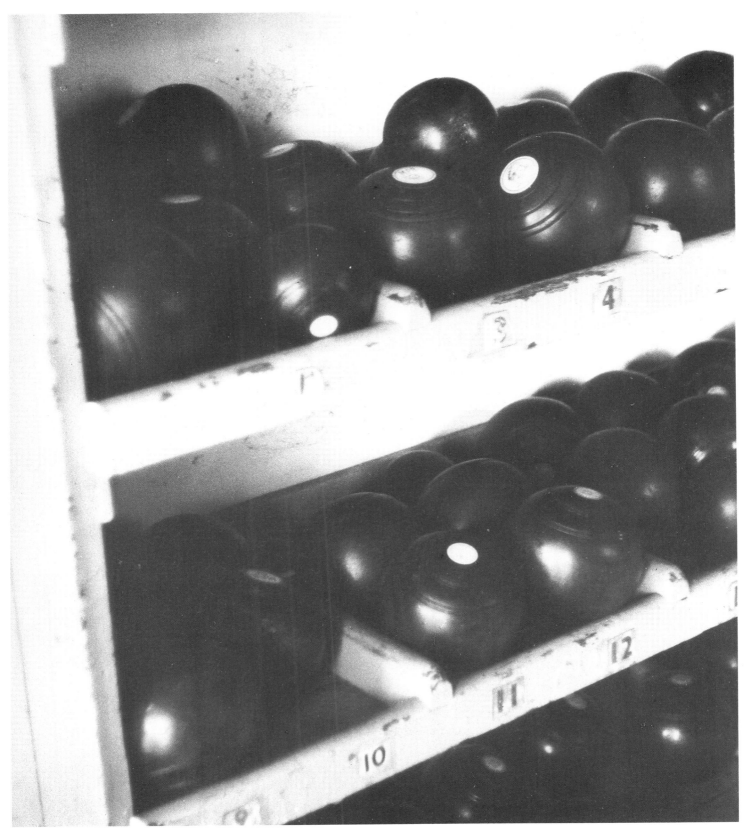

Myrtle Park, Bingley

37

West Bowling, Bradford

"There is no public house in Saltaire. Thus, with comfortable houses and every inducement to stay at home – with literary and social institutions in their very midst, with high-class tastes, and, to crown all, a beautiful temple to the worship of God – it would be strange indeed had Saltaire not a reputation and a name. The erection of baths and wash-houses has been a great advance. Cleanliness is the greatest condition of health: whilst the removal of whole masses of damp clothes from the streets, and of the steam of washing-tubs from the houses, greatly conduces to the health and comfort of the inhabitants. Indoor washing is most pernicious, and a fruitful source of disease, especially to the young.

To get rid of consumption from the disease list is almost, if not quite, impossible. Where persons of different temperament, constitutional vigour, and age, often carelessly clothed, leave home early in the morning, generally without partaking of food, and this, too in our irregular and often inclement climate, consumption must and will result. The question involved is rather one that rests upon the people themselves, than one in which masters can interfere. The workpeople can only be taught that warm clothing instead of finery, good food, and regular hours, combined with home sanitary regulations, are necessary to keep down this terrible malady.

extracts from the Medical Report submitted to
the Imperial Commission on Saltaire 1867

Saltaire

But ah didn't feel i' onny better sperrits as ah went hoam, 'cos it war hailin' and blawin' like mad; an' if Bella worn't lewkin' aht for me to goa an lewk at them hens, 'cos they'd laid noa eggs for three days an' shoo wor sewer they wor poarly. Shoo'd putten one on 'em on t'rug afore t'fire 'cos shoo said it lewkt starved to deeath. Well, that thear hen, sitha, it shook it feathers at me, an' it put it heead o' one side an' it oppened it beeak, an' it said as plain as it could speyk 'at it wor noan bahn to lay eggs for a bloated capitalist like me, an' it wor bahn for stick aht for nationalism.

from an *Abe Clegg talk (Among the Pessimists)*
(first published 1918-22 by
The Yorkshire Post)

Boulder Clough, near Luddenden Foot

40

Sowerby Bridge

Eventide

Three slahces o' breead on a
     plate;
Three slahces o' breead cut
     thick
Taks sum gettin daahn
When a chap's sick.

Bahdin' in t'owd men's hoam;
Lahf's wark nearly dun;
Cum to think on t'Jonty lad,
T'battles nearly wun.

Lig him daahn on his sheet-
     swaddled bed;
Smooith his pillow straight;
Put his pension-book at hand,
Other things can wait.

Three slahces o' breead on a
     plate;
Three slahces o' breead cut
     thick;
Poor tack' fer a wastin'
     soul,
Cum a chap's sick.

by Fred Brown from a collection of his
     poems, *The Muse Went Weaving*
     (published by the Yorkshire Dialect Society)

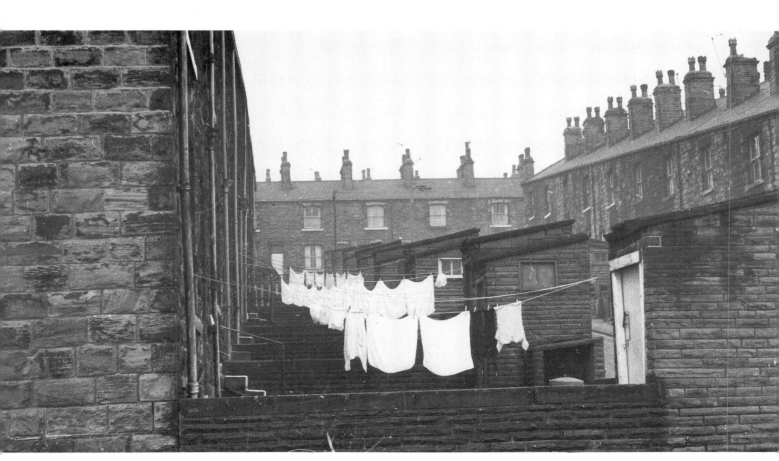

Back Oxford Street, East Ardsley, near Wakefield

John Street, Crossflatts, near Bingley

Colne Valley, near Marsden

The inhabitants of Ossett, a village three miles from Wakefield, have been employed in making broad woollen cloth from time out of mind. In this year (1734) the weavers &c, employed in that trade had to work fifteen hours every day for eightpence. A horn was blown at five o'clock in the morning, the time for beginning, and at eight at night, the time for leaving work. The clothiers had to take their goods to Leeds to sell, and had to stand in Briggate in all sorts of weather. About the year 1736, Richard Wilson, a resident of Ossett, made two pieces of broad cloth; he carried them on his head to Leeds and sold it – the merchant being in want of the fellow piece, he went from Leeds to Ossett, then carried the other piece to Leeds, and then walked to Ossett again; he walked about forty miles that day.

from *The Annals and History of Leeds*
compiled by John Mayhall (1860)

Siddal, Halifax

Nay, shut that doar, it's rare an
    cowd toneet,
Draw up to t'hob an wahm thi
    frozzen feet.
There's t'havercake o' t'breead-
    fleck hengin up,
Wilt hev a bite wi me an just a
    sup?
It's cowd, Ah knaw. Sam up that
    fire-point, Luke,
Poke aht them asses into
    t'assenook.
There's t'kettle singin! What if
    t'neet be dree,
We'll sooin be wahm. Ah'll brew a
    pot o'tea.

from *An Anthology of West Riding Dialect
    Verse* W.J. Halliday (published 1964
    by the Yorkshire Dialect Society)

Penny Hill, near Stainland, Elland

46

"Formerly (the early part of the 19th Century) every weaver was really a manufacturer or master clothier. His dyeing-pan, which was of lead, was set out of doors. Such men would go to Huddersfield, buy their 50lbs weight of wool, carry it home on their backs, spread it out on the house floor, sprinkle it with oil, layer on layer, then beat it with sticks. Hand cards were then used. They teased it together, and turned it off in a floss state, as they do now by the scribbling machine. They worked it together in long slivings; it was then spun into rough or fine threads, then into warp and woof.

"The piece when made was spread on the floor. A large kitful of urine and swine's dung was taken and strained through straw: it was then sprinkled on the cloth, and, as may be imagined, the smell in the house was horrible. As they lecked one piece it was layed down, and so layer on layer were placed in the form of a long parallelogram raised from the ground; then all the members of the household got up and trampled on it. There it lay until morning; it was then wrapped up in a bundle, taken to Honley (or the nearest place) to a fulling mill; it was scoured, the offensive fluid washed out of it, and it was then brought dripping home. It was next trailed over furze bushes, hung out upon the walls, and the small pieces pulled off in the bushes whisked from it; then burled in the house by the family.

"It was then taken again to the mill and placed in the fulling stocks with soap, by which process it was reduced in dimensions. It was afterwards laid on the mill-stone (a long stone table) and stamped by the Government official, who affixed seals to the piece impressed with the length and breadth. It was then carried home, and as it was being fastened to the tenter, the family pulled at one end to increase the length. If it was stamped, say for 50 yards, it would thus stretch to fifty-one or fifty-two, and shrink again on being finished. The market was at Huddersfield and the cloth was exposed for sale on the Church-yard wall.

Colne Valley, near Slaithwaite

"The seals, before spoken of, were of lead. The officer, who was sworn at Pontefract Sessions, made a hole at each end of the piece. A strip of lead three and a half inches long and a half an inch broad was bended at one end; it was passed through the cloth, and by means of a hole at one end of the lead and a button at the other, it was rivetted with a hammer. The length was stamped on the lead with a die. The manufacturer was now at liberty to remove his cloth, which before could not have been done under a fine. This stamp law became obsolete twenty or thirty years before it was repealed."

from *The History of Huddersfield*
Taylor Dyson M.A. (published 1932)
quoting a book by the Rev. A. Easther, former
headmaster of King James' Grammar School.

Colne Road, near Stanbury, Haworth

Outlane Moor, near Huddersfield

Denholme Beck, Denholme

By 1835, Horsfall and Co. (Bradford) had 378 power looms in their worsted mill, and in Yorkshire as a whole the picture was as follows:

Power Looms in use in 1835

Woollen	Woollen and Worsted	Woollen and Cotton	Worsted
688	226	307	2,856

The following table, based on the prices paid by a Bolton master to his hand-loom weavers, indicates the distress which mechanisation brought to this section of the working class:

Price for a piece of cloth (24 yards long) approximately a week's work for a handloom weaver:

1777 – 1803	. . .	£1	6s 8d
1804 – 1810	. . .	£1	0s 0d
1811 – 1817	. . .		14s 7d
1818 – 1824	. . .		8s 9d
1825 – 1831	. . .		6s 4d
1832 – 1853	. . .		5s 6d

from *Industrial Revolution in Yorkshire*
Fred Singleton (published 1970)

River Holme, Huddersfield

Canal near Wakefield Road, Huddersfield

Canal, Todmorden

Will, qualified as a carpenter, was promoted to chargehand, foreman and eventually length foreman for the stretch between Silsden and Leeds. Most of his working life was spent on the area of the cut . . .

I asked him if in building lock gates he followed James Brindley's plans and this stimulated another fascinating story.

"We followed no plans at all," he insisted with twinkling eyes, "we simply replaced the existing gates. Apart from one lock at St. Anns Ing near Leeds, which for some obscure reason was made wider than all the others, the gates were of standard width, 10ft 2ins, but no two pairs were alike."

"The replacing of the gates worked on a yearly programme," he added, "making the gates indoors during the winter months and doing the fixing or hanging during the summer. The timber for the gates was sawn into logs and stood in the timber yard for at least four years to get thoroughly seasoned. It was English oak of best quality – knots, shakes and sap were taboo. The actual making of the gates was all done by hand; the deep mortices in the heel and mitre posts were all worked out by first boring a series of holes and then chiselled out by hand, using great big paring chisels as big as a cricket bat. My own set of chisels were over a hundred years old and are now in Stanley Bridges' museum, Sheffield.

"The gates lasted for anything between twenty-five years for gate heads and forty to fifty for others. The record must be held, I think, by a pair which are still working in the Five-Rise, which were fixed in 1911. We made gates for the whole of the Yorkshire area, and I helped make and hang about sixty pairs, so there are still a lot in use from my times."

from *Slow Boat Through Pennine Waters*
Frederick Doerflinger (published 1971)

Bingley from the Five Rise Locks

Tow-path, Luddenden Foot

Sometimes in summer, when the mornings are fine, I make a detour on my way to work and go by way of the canal.

I like canals; I like the spirit of them. They refuse to be tied down to the staid convention of two parallel lines; they adorn themselves with verdure in the most unexpected places.

They are placid – not having the quick urgency of rivers – which suits the mood of the morning.

I always remember my first trip on the canal. It was a Sunday School outing, and a party of excited children assembled at the lock to board a brightly painted barge which had been swabbed and scrubbed. The motive force was the power of one horse, but that sturdy animal was equal to the task.

The business of the locks at once fascinated and frightened me, but when the first one was negotiated confidence was established. Some small boys grew bolder and hung perilously inverted on the side of the barge, but happily no-one tumbled in.

from an article by Fred Brown in
The Huddersfield Examiner, Sept. 16th 1953

58

The main line of the canal (the Calder-Hebble) was completed about 1772 and the Salterhebble to Sowerby Bridge stretch in 1747 . . . Smeaton's canal was a sound straightforward piece of work, introducing no trick engineering such as swing aqueducts or tunnels where the boatman lay on his back and propelled the vessel by walking like a fly on the ceiling. A tow path ran alongside the canal, and the proverbially silly boat horse dragged the barge of some three feet draught along . . .

The crews of the vessels were nomadic bargees who lived with their families on the boat, the women working as hard as the men, often steering or even drawing along the tow path. They patronised the various "Navigation" Inns on the route, and were often difficult to locate. After the introduction of compulsory education it seemed impossible to get the bargee's children to attend any school.

from an article by W.B. Trigg from
The Centenary Book of Halifax (1948)

Canal depot, Leeds

Sir John Ramsden's Canal, Fartown, Huddersfield

Th'canal banks wor like a carpet o' breet colours – an th'river ran below, – shaded wi' trees under which th'ground seemed covered wi' a claad ov hyacinths. Th'sweetest scents wor wafted throo ivvery side – May blossoms wor soa thick on some o' th'thorn trees wol they lukt as if they'd been in a snow storm. Rolling hills stretched far away on awther side, covered wi' cottages 'at seemed th'picturs ov content. We sat daan to admire an' drink it all an' for the first time sin leaving hooam aw felt thankful at awd come.

from *Seets I'Yorkshire and Lancashire*
(Grimes' comical trip from Leeds to
Liverpool by canal), John Hartley (1916)

Canal, Marsden

Water Haigh Colliery, Rothwell

I'm collier Jack, through Wibsey Slack, am allus praad to tell
'At few fairs in old England, can Wibsey Slack excel;
There's plenty raam for cattle and other sports we share,
I'm allus praad to go wi' my mates, to t'seets at Wibsey fair.

Chorus:
So cheer up, my collier lads, an' niver forget to share
The jolly fun for old and young, at t'seets of Wibsey fair.

At Wibsey fair we gladly share, we've cake an' beef an' ale,
With strangers too, as weel as friends, we're nivver known to fail;
There's English, Irish, Scotch and Welsh, and ivvery other mak
That likes to come and see wer fun at top o' Wibsey Slack.

Chorus: So cheer up, my collier lads, etc.

There's Bruffile and ther Irish tits through Dublin and Kildare,
Al back thes nought to lik ther show that comes to Wibsey fair,
For farming wark or carriage drive, or any hunting track,
Yo can please yersen at ony price, at top o' Wibsey Slack.

Chorus: So cheer up, my collier lads, etc.

There's Boxing Shows and Comic Shows and swinging boats as well;
Thes quacks donned up i' the soldier clothes, their physic for to sell.
I'll bet they cure you on the spot, if you believe their tales,
But ad rather chonce a lump o' beef and a drop of good old Wibsey ale.

Chorus: So cheer up, my collier lads, etc.

There's sharpers looking out for flats to see what they can catch,
Thes bobbies donned up i' plain clothes at's sharp upon ther track.
They know em by the style they cut, while looking out to snare
The country lads and lasses at goes wi' t'brass to spend at Wibsey fair.

Chorus: So cheer up, my collier lads, etc.

So here's success to Wibsey Slack, the place where I were born,
Ther foolish folks, at often tries to run it doun with scorn;
But I love the birth-place and my mates, that's honest, true and square,
As nivver forget the jolly fun I've had at Wibsey fair.

Chorus: So cheer up, my collier lads, an' niver forget to share
         The jolly fun for old and young, at t'seets of Wibsey fair.

An old folk-song (*circa* mid 19th Century)
from *Illustrated Rambles from Hipperholme
to Tong,* James Parker (published 1904)

Water Haigh Colliery, Rothwell

North Gawber Colliery, Barnsley

A collier lad, a collier lad,
  A collier lad for me, O.
He works in a hole as black as the coal,
  And brings all his brass home to me, O.

He says: Sithee, lass, Ah've browt thi me brass,
  Ah'll nivver get drunk ony more, O.
Ah'll save all me brass and buy a jackass
  And ride past the ale-house door, O.

a West Riding mining ballad
from a collection compiled by A.L. Lloyd entitled
Come All Ye Bold Miners (published 1952)

The nature of the occurrence, but not its frightful extent, was immediately known in the neighbourhood, and the inmates – frantic wives and weeping children of the colliery dwellings, rushed in almost utter despair towards the pit head. The shrieks and wailings of these poor creatures were most heart rending, and the scene of mental anguish which was displayed in various forms is almost beyond conception, and can never be forgotten by even the most unreflecting spectator who was present . . .

Search was made by relays of miners until all the living were got out; but some time after that, about twelve o'clock at night, a voice was heard calling, "Wo hoy, wo hoy!" Making way to the spot whence the sounds came from the men found a young man called Balgue who was without a bruise and had suffered very little from the fire-damp. He was of considerable use in showing the drifts of the mine etc., to the strange workmen who were so laudably exerting themselves to save human life, and also to remove the bodies of the unfortunate dead. On Balgue being discovered, the men had their hopes risen to expect that they would find more of the workmen alive; but alas! vain were the hopes. The death-blast had passed on its fatal course and 73 human souls in a moment had been called from time to eternity!

from a report in the *Leeds Intelligencer* about an explosion at Oaks Colliery near Barnsley (March 13th, 1847)

Sixteen men lost their lives and eight were injured in an explosion which occurred at North Gawber Colliery near Barnsley this evening.

The explosion occurred about two hours after the afternoon shift had begun work and about 60 miners were in the affected area. Along the coal face there were three cutting machines, and a considerable number of men were at the other end of the face. The explosion occurred where the largest number of men were working. The seam is only about 2ft. 9in. high and normally the men work in a prone position or crouched on their haunches. It was in this position that they were caught by the explosion. The fact that they were in such a shallow seam added to their difficulties, but fortunately they had not far to go before they came to much higher roadway. Choked with dust which filled the working places, severely burnt by the flames, many of them with their clothing alight, they had to crawl on their hands and knees to safety.

from a report in *The Times* about an explosion at North Gawber Colliery (September 13th 1935)

St. Gabriel's Church, East Ardsley, near Wakefield

Shops were all closed and ivverybody, oud and young, had a haliday aat oth doors, for they wor all flade a missin the Grand Processhun wich form itsel at th top o Wutheren, wich wen it wor meshured, it turn'd aat to be two miles six inches long – it moved as follows.

ORDER OF PROCESSION

The Springhead Band wi' their hat bruads turn'd
up so as they mud see their way clear
Lord et Manor i' full uniform a fut back bearing
Coat of Arms for Haworth,

Haworth Station

68

a gert wild cratur wi two tails on, one at athur end.
Two citizens wi white cravats raund their hats,
Th Members et Corporashun one abreast
singing' "a nuttin we will go brave boys."
Big drums and Triangles
A Mahogany Wheelbarrow and a silver trowel on a
cart trail'd wi six donkeys, and garded wi
ten lazy policemen all sober.
A pair of crackt bag-pipes.
The Contractor in a sedan carried wi two waggoners
in white smocks.
All th' young maidens fra fourteen to thirty nine,
six abreast, drest i sky blue, and singin
throo combs.
Twenty navvies i their shirt sleeves wheeling
barrows wi work toils in.
Taan skavengers wi shoulder'd Berzums
decorated wi ribbons.
Bellman and Pinder arm i arm drest i full uniform
and latter na and then bawlin aat wats
baun to tak place.
All scholars ath female line laking at duck under
water kit, and th' males laking at frog-loup,
and jumping o one another's backs.
Taan chimla sweeps maunted o donkeys wi their
faces white.
All the furinners fra th'continent o Haworth,
and crookt legg'd uns fra Keighley
follow'd up.
Bulk oth inhabitants walkin one abreast
wi their hats off.

from *Th'History of Haworth Railway Fro
t'Beginnin' t' th'end*
Bill o' th'Hoylus End (William Wright)
(a pamphlet printed in Keighley 1867)

Lockwood Station, Huddersfield

She squeezed his arm. "Josh, lad, why don't you go next Saturday to hear Mr. Carl Halle's theatre orchestra at Manchester? Your father'd noan mind you having the afternoon off for once in a while, and I've heard that the railway is running at two-and-six for gentlemen."

from *The Crowthers of Bankdam*
Thomas Armstrong (published 1940)

70

Hewenden Viaduct, Cullingworth

You've heeard tell abaat th'new railroad aw dar say?
It's an age o' steam is this! Smook nuisance and
boilers brustin are ivery-day affairs, an' ivery thing
an' ivery body seem to be on at full speed. Aw
wonder 'at noabody invents a man wi a drivin
pulley at is back soa's they could speed him up as
they do a loom to soa mony picks a minut; th'chap
'at gets a patent for that ul mak a fortun.

from *Yorkshire Puddin' (Th' New Railroad)*
John Hartley (published 1877)

71

Passage under railway, Dewsbury

Lockwood Viaduct, Huddersfield

Halifax Station

I remember one Saturday in May 1853, when I was in charge of the last passenger train from Huddersfield, due to leave Bradford at 11.10 p.m. On arriving at Low Moor the engine broke down, and the driver said it could not be moved from the main line. In those days all engines were stabled at Mirfield, and there was no telegraphic communication. The station master said there would be no engine available until nine o'clock on Sunday morning. The passengers, numbering about thirty would have to walk to Bradford, a distance of over four miles.

Seeing it was midnight, I said that it was too bad to have to walk. "Have you no shunt horses about?" He replied that they had been turned into the field hours ago, not being wanted until Monday. I then asked him to send one of the platform porters for one and told him to bring it to the station harnessed, which he did. We then put all the passengers into a third-class carriage which was fitted up with a good outside brake. The horse was yoked in front of the carriage, with a man in charge of it. I took charge of the carriage brake, and off we went to Bradford about midnight.

The horse pulled the carriage on the line through the dark Low Moor tunnel, which is over a 1000 yards long, and brought the carriage to a stand at the top of the incline going to Bradford, a distance of over two miles. He was then detached from the carriage and taken back through the tunnel to Low Moor. I then took the carriage down the descending gradient of 1 in 50 over a mile long into the station at Bradford, arriving there safely about one o'clock on Sunday morning. The passengers assembled on the platform and gave me three good hearty cheers. This was the second time I had been honoured with cheers by the passengers on arriving at Bradford station.

from *The Lancashire and Yorkshire Railway*
Thomas Normington (District Superintendent
for Yorkshire Section), (published 1898)

Hebden Bridge

He had by now descended to the level of the stream crossed the wooden footbridge, and was mounting the other side of the valley. The narrow lane was certainly very difficult; round stones were scattered loosely over its surface, and this morning they were all white with rime, and very slippery. The rough grass by the lane's rim, too, was thickly white, and here and there across the track sheets of ice lay gleaming. But it was a glorious morning, just at the very edge where winter turns to spring; the sun was not very high, and the Oldroyd's side of the valley lay in deep shadow, but as Will mounted up towards Scape Scar he came out into the clear February sunshine.

from *Inheritance* Phyllis Bentley
(published 1931)

Booth Bank, Slaithwaite

Steep Lane, near Sowerby Village

Away towards Lancashire swept the dry heather-land and peat, billow on billow, till the desolate edge of the sky was gained; then came the wet land, where the bog had not grown to a head as yet – where it was filling, as the moor folk say; and below that again there was Hawkhill Bog, twisting like a lake of pitch around the foot of the Lonely Valley. To the right of the bridle-path ran a streamway, through which the water slipped, with a curious lithe noiselessness, between the banks of peat. And it was a thing to make a man's blood run cold, this deep silence of the water – the water which is the last thing in all nature to hold its voice for awe.

from *Ricroft of Withens*
Halliwell Sutcliffe (published 1898)

Nichol's Yard, Sowerby Bridge

Hallas Bridge Mill, Cullingworth

Loom Harmony

Clickerty-Clack, Clackerty-Clack,
    Shuttle and bobbin,
Clickerty-Clack, Clackerty-Clack,
    Mary Jane's sobbin'.
T'tuner's upbraided her,
    Sho's forgettun to oil:
Clickerty-Clack, Clackerty-Clack,
    Mullock and moil.

Mucky Weft

Ah wonder, ah is it
At faults made i'weyving
Show fifty tahms waar
When they get up to t'perch:
Ther's plenty'll be capt
When they get across t'border,
And finnd at ther faults
Weren't mended in t'church.

from *Yorkshire Dialect Poems* 1914-
    1943, Fred Brown (published
    by the Yorkshire Dialect
    Society 1943)

River Calder, Hebden Bridge

One day he wor at t'beckside, an' shoo went to see what he wor dooin', an' as shoo saw he'd nobbut one clog, shoo axed him what he'd done wi' tother, an' he sed he'd made it into a booat, an' it had sailed away down t'beck, soa shoo tawked nicely, an' tell'd him he shouldn't do soa, for it wor lost, an' he mud allus remember 'at if he put owt into t'beck, he'd niver see it ony moor, for t'watter ran daan at sich a rate; but he sed he'd fun aght a better way o' dooin' it next time, for he'd put t' furst in wi"t' toa pointin daan t'hill, but when he put t'next in, he'd point t'toa up t'hill, an' it wouldn't find it quite soa easy goin.

"A'a, Sammy lad," sed his mother, as shoo stroked his heead, "tha's a deal moor i'this nop not ivver thi fayther had, or me awther, for aw should niver ha' throwt o' that."

Sammy put tother in, takkin care to point t'toe t'contrary way to what t'watter wor runnin, but as soon as he left lawse it turned raand an' foller'd tother, an' wor sooin aght o' seet.

"Nah, then!" he sed "didn't aw tell you? If it hadn't turned raand, it 'ud ha' been goin' up t'hill, but t'chap 'at made them clogs didn't mak' 'em reeights an' lefts. You see they're booath left, an' aw believe that's the reason aw' we allus been lat to t'schooil."

from *Yorkshire Puddin'*
John Hartley (published 1877)
from the chapter "Sammy Bewitched"

Marsden

Hallas Bridge Mill, Cullingworth

Little by little, as the superiority of the new methods became too obvious for the most bigoted mill-owner to ignore, innovations were made; the mill-wheel gave place to the engine, and the hideous chimney rose from the hillside or above the tree-tops in the valley, and belched forth its black smoke in mockery of the stream whose office it had usurped; but until inconvenience was to the breaking-point, and removal or ruin became the alternative, the old mills on the banks of the brooks were not abandoned.

Right up to the time of his death Mr. Middleton's father had been content with water power. The Upper Mill had been built in the heart of the wood, a mile away from the village by the field path, and even more by the crooked and stony lane over which the drays had to travel. The Valley Mill, however, was only a stone's-throw from the bridge and the dwellings of the "hands", though until the round chimney was erected you might never have suspected its presence, as it was almost concealed by a rising mound on the one side and a thick screen of trees on the other.

But when the younger man came into possession he had not hesitated to make friends with the new power, and had promptly put an engine into the Valley Mill and run his looms by steam. He had been urged to this course not so much by competition – because at that time competition did not affect him very much – as by the practical difficulty of maintaining a constant water supply. In the case of the Upper Mill his experiences had been less irritating; and partly on that account, in part also because he had felt that he was making some concessions to the spirit of his father; and again – though in much less degree – because it had seemed to him a "beastly shame" to put a chimney in such a romantic spot and to do away with the mill-race which had seized his imagination when a boy, he still utilised water-power for his drawing-frames and spinning jennies. But he would have gone out of business altogether rather than forsake the Upper Mill with its early and cherished associations.

from *The Way of the Winepress*
W. Riley (published 1917)

Stanbury, near Haworth

Denholme

Thornton Parish Church, near Skipton

Weavers' cottages, Booth Bank, near Slaithwaite

1825 February 3rd: The septennial festival in honour of Bishop Blaize was celebrated at Bradford with unusual splendour. As it appears probable that the honours then paid to the wool-combers' Saint will be the last of the kind rendered here, it will be interesting to give an account of the ceremony. The weather being very fine, at an early hour in the morning the surrounding towns and villages began to pour in their population. About eight o'clock in the morning the persons intending to form part of the procession began to assemble in Westgate; and shortly before ten o'clock under the superintendence of Mathew Thompson Esq., were formed in the following order:–

Herald bearing the flag.

24 Woolstaplers on horseback, each horse caparisoned with a fleece.

38 Worsted Spinners on horseback, in white stuff waistcoats, with each a sliver of wool over his shoulder and a white stuff sash: the horses' necks covered with nets made of thick yarn.

6 Merchants on horseback, with coloured sashes.

3 Guards. Masters' colours. 3 Guards.

56 Apprentices and Masters' Sons on horseback, with ornamental caps, scarlet stuff coats, white stuff waistcoats, and blue pantaloons.

Bradford & Keighley Bands.

Mace bearer, on foot.

6 Guards. KING. QUEEN. 6 Guards.

Jason – Princess Medea.

Guards

Bishop's chaplain.

BISHOP BLAIZE

Shepherd and Shepherdesses.

Shepherd Swains.

160 Woolsorters on horseback, with ornamented caps, and various coloured slivers.

30 Comb Makers.

Charcoal Burners.

Combers' Colours.

Band.

470 Woolcombers, with wool wigs, etc.

Band.

40 Dyers, with red cockades, blue aprons, and crossed slivers of red and blue.

from *The Annals and History of Leeds*
compiled by John Mayhall (1860)

Micklethwaite, near Bingley

Bulrush Mill, Batley

It was now the middle of the month of February; by six o'clock therefore, dawn was just beginning to steal on night, to penetrate with a pale ray its brown obscurity, and give a demi-translucency to its opaque shadows. Pale enough that ray was on this particular morning; no colour tinged the east, no flush warmed it. To see what a heavy lid slowly lifted, what a wan glance she flung along the hills, you would have thought the sun's fire quenched in last night's floods. The breath of the morning was chill as its aspect; a raw wind stirred the mass of night-cloud, and showed, as it slowly rose – leaving a colourless, silver-gleaming ring all round the horizon – not blue sky, but a stratum of paler vapour beyond. It had ceased to rain, but the earth was sodden, and the pools and rivulets were full.

The mill-windows were alight, the bell rung loud, and now the little children came running in, in too great a hurry, let us hope, to feel very much nipped by the inclement air; and, indeed, by contrast, perhaps the morning appeared rather favourable to them than otherwise; for they had often come to their work in winter, through snow-storms, through heavy rain, through hard frost.

from *Shirley*
Charlotte Brontë (published 1849)

Longbottom's Mill, Sowerby Bridge

Average age of death (early 19th Century)

	Gentry, Manufacturers etc.	Tradesmen Shopkeepers	Labourers Mill operators
Leeds	44 years	27 years	19 years
Halifax	55 years	24 years	22 years

from *Industrial Revolution in Yorkshire*
Fred Singleton (published 1970)

Crib Lane, Halifax

"Take your hat," said he. "Take what belongs to you, and go out of that door; get away to your parish, you pauper: beg, steal, starve, get transported, do what you like; but at your peril venture again into my sight! If ever I hear of your setting foot on an inch of ground belonging to me, I'll hire a man to cane you."

I thought only of walking, that the action of my muscles might harmonise with the action of my nerves; and walk I did, fast and far. How could I do otherwise? A load was lifted off my heart; I felt light and liberated. I had got away from Bigben Close without a breach of resolution; without injury to my self-respect. I had not forced circumstances; circumstances had freed me. Life was again open to me; no longer was its horizon limited by the high black wall surrounding Crimsworth's mill. Two hours had elapsed before my sensations had so far subsided as to leave me calm enough to remark for what wider and clearer boundaries I had exchanged my sooty girdle. When I did look up, lo! straight before me lay Grovetown, a village of villas about five miles out of X——. The short winter day, as I perceived from the far-declined sun, was already approaching its close; a chill frost-mist was rising from the river on which X—— stands, and along whose banks the road I had taken lay; it dimmed the earth, but did not obscure the clear icy blue of the January sky. There was a great stillness near and far; the time of the day favoured tranquillity, as the people were all employed within doors, the hour of evening release from the factories not being yet arrived; a sound of full-flowing water alone pervaded the air, for the river was deep and abundant, swelled by the melting of a late snow.

from *The Professor*
Charlotte Brontë (published 1853)

Near City Road, Bradford

Hey Street, Listerhills, Bradford

Mill at Ripponden

Elland

If you miln pieces reit,
An' you cuttle 'em streit,
  An' finish 'em fit for to wear,
Then yor wage sud be good
An yor wark sewerly sud
  Not leave yo o'er burdened wi
    care.

from *Heavy Woollen District*
Textile Workers Union
Ben Turner (published 1917)

If you spin yarn at's true,
Whether brahn, black or blue,
  To mak into fine cloth bi'th mass,
Ye owt to be happy,
An' nivver made snappy,
  Becos yon been crippled for
    brass.

If you weyve cloth correct,
Yon a reit to expect,
  A decent reward; it's what's due.
It's easy to win it,
Soa let us begin it,
  And each to each other be true.

Weaving is a simple job with power-looms, and an easier; that is all. But, bless me, with hand-looms it was horse-work. There are cotton weavers in Lancashire that think they are punished because they have to stand more nor eight hours in a day and see their work done for them. Why, we thought little in them days of tewing away, week in and week out, for fourteen and fifteen hours, taking our meals where we sat. And even at that, a man that wave in his own house sometimes wrought all night to finish his piece so as he could set off with it at daylight on his shoulder, a tramp of three or four miles over the moor. He brought back, happen, three or four shillings in his pocket, and another warp; and then took his bit of sleep by daylight.

"Horse-work" have I written? Horses are better done by. I ponder on it, and I hardly credit what I know to be true. It is not to tell how men lived so. In December, I think, we did a fortnight's work hand-running, and the weavers, fancying there would be more when that was done, went at it right manfully. It was all good-paying stuff, but heavy to weave – a camlet cloth, needing weighted slay-boards. I gat a share of it, in place of one that was laid at home badly, I know not that I ever devoured work with such gluttony as I did that. After the first two days it seemed as if I could not tire. When we went to it of a morning, the smell of the shop made me keen; and all day the din of the looms clacking and bumping set me merry. They faced all one way, the length of a narrow chamber, and I could look along and see the others belting it. But to my thinking we were never fairly agate till after dark, when we had lighted candles, and the shop was throng with great, dithering shadows. By that time we had done talking, and no matter what weather it was, a steam ran down the windows.

from *Web of An Old Weaver*
J. Keighley Snowden (published 1896)

Bingley

"But I've taken the oath," he told himself again firmly:

"It's too late to change my mind now." The thought of the oath reminded him of the paper he held in his hand, and he felt a sharp curiosity to know its terms. He hesitated on Mary's account, lest he should disturb her, but could not forbear lighting the candle and reading. The oath was well written, in a clerkly pointed script; Joe wondered whose hand it was, and whether it had come from Nottingham.

I, A.B. of my own voluntary will, he read, do declare and solemnly swear, that I never will reveal to any person or persons, under the canopy of heaven, the names of the persons who compose this secret committee, their proceedings, meetings, places of abode, dress, features, complexion, or anything else that might lead to a discovery of the same, either by word, deed or sign, under the penalty of being sent out of the world by the first brother that shall meet me, and my name and character blotted out of existence, and never to be remembered but with contempt and abhorrence; and I further now do swear, that I will use my best endeavours to punish by death any traitor or traitors, should any rise up amongst us, wherever I can find him or them, and though he should fly to the verge of nature, I will pursue him with unceasing vengeance. So help me God, and bless me to keep this my oath inviolable.

" 'Punish by death!" mused Joe. "That's strong! 'Unceasing vengeance!' I don't know that I should have sworn if it had been this oath George'd given me."

There was a light noise behind him; he started round to find Mary standing at the bottom of the stairs.

"I'm sorry I wakened thee, lass," said Joe, looking at her with commiseration, for in this half light she had a wearied and troubled air, and her rosy cheeks looked pale.

Mary came towards him at the table, picked up a candle and held it to his face. After a moment she set it down again.

"Tha's sworn, Joe," she said, her lovely voice sad and low.

"I knew tha would."

"I were very sorry for t'croppers I couldn't help it," said Joe wretchedly.

from *Inheritance*
Phyllis Bentley (published 1931)

Park Works, Bradford Road, Batley

"Keep yer eye on that door, Vic, when yer talkin', an' t'minnit ye see it oppen shut yer mouth up an' turn to yer piece. If it's nobbut an ovverlooker or Joss ye've no 'casion to bother, but if it chances to be t'boss 'e'll maker yer 'air curl for ye."

from *The Way of the Winepress*
W. Riley (published 1917)

Baxter Lane, Northowram, near Halifax

"So you've gotten t'wind again, have you?" said Mrs. Crowther grimly. "You get it every time you eat hot oven-cake. Hurry up, lass . . . no, t'copper kettle."

The sufferer sipped the steaming water, had a further supply and then belched freely. He, holding up his hand, anticipated the coming scolding. "Alreet, alreet, it's my own fault. But I fair can't resist your oven-cakes, Lydia." From the nail on the wall he removed the large key. "Get your shawl on, lass," he said, belching again, "while I go down to the privy to get shut on the rest o' this."

"That reminds me, Simeon," said Mrs. Crowther. "You must see about getting the cesspool cleared out. What with one thing an' another I forgot to mention it."

"Stinks, does it?" nodded Mr. Crowther. From a shelf he took a stubby, clay pipe, the mouthpiece of which was bound with cotton thread, and filled it with shreds of black tobacco he cut from a bar he held in the palm of his hand. Lighting a spill he applied it to the bowl, and sucked out the strong fumes.

"Get out of here wi' that," cried Mrs. Crowther, coughing.

Her husband laughed. "I'll noan be able to niff the stinks in the privy with this wi' me," he said. "You should start smoking, lass."

He snatched a piece of old newspaper, climbed the steps into the wash-kitchen, clumped across the flagged floor, and opened the back door.

from *The Crowthers of Bankdam*
Thomas Armstrong (published 1940)

Spring Garden Street, Queensbury

Stoney Royd Terrace, Whitegate, Halifax

Joshua Street, where I was born, is made of Yorkshire stone. Smoke and the weather have turned the walls black like the rocks on the bare Pennine hills around, and the face of each stone bulges out, giving a serrated effect like a crocodile's back. The street, with its cobble-like pavement, looks reptilian, and being most of the time wet with mist and rain its amphibian appearance is emphasized. It is clean, well drained, and the flags have been worn smooth by the energetic swilling and scouring of the women, as well as by the iron tread of their clogs. When for short periods the sun comes out the worn stone glows with warm, mellow tints. Not a speck of dirt is to be seen. At night the street is lit by two green-painted iron gas-lamps.

During the day the street is pervaded with the throbbing of near-by factories and the faint chatter of looms, a continuous monotonous sound broken only by the chirping of sparrows and violent outbursts of noise from the railway.

In the morning, at dinner-time, and in the evening weavers, spinners, and other cotton workers clatter along the street in their iron-shod clogs. Six days of the week smoke rises from the factory chimneys and steam rises from the neighbouring grates in the streets, where weft-skips, boxes, and wooden beams with iron flanges are stacked high, and all the time warm water flows from the factories into the canal. On Saturday morning at half-past eleven the droning note of machinery in the town sinks gradually into silence and the working folk go home to wash and dress up for the week-end. The womenfolk come out in the afternoon with shopping-baskets covered with white crochet-work cloths to visit shops and the pagoda-like stalls on the little market ground, while most of the men go to football or cricket matches. On Sunday the shops are closed and the town enjoys a quiet Sabbath, silent save for the pealing of church-bells and the organ-led singing in the chapels.

from *I Haven't Unpacked* (An Autobiography)
William Holt (published 1939)

"A gooid way to stop a chap's maath is to keep yer own shut."

"A chap 'at's liberal wi' advice is generally niggardly wi'
'is brass."

"Ther's some born fooils, an' ther's some mak thersen fooils,
an' ther's some get made fooils on."

Three sayings by John Hartley

Hainworth Lane, Springbank, Keighley

Wood Terrace, Primrose Hill, Huddersfield

The Old Weaver's Lament

Chorus

Poverty poverty knock,
My loom is a-saying all day;
Poverty poverty knock,
Gaffer's too skinny to pay;
Poverty poverty knock,
Keeping one eye on the clock;
I know I can guttle
When I hear my shuttle
Go Poverty poverty knock.

Verses

Up every morning at five,
Ah wonder that we keep alive;
Tired and yawning
On the cold morning,
It's back to the old dreary drive.
Oh dear we're going to be late,
Gaffer is stood at the gate;
We're out of pocket,
Our wages they've dockit,
We have to buy grub on the slate.
Oh dear my poor 'ead it sings,
I should've a-woven three strings,
But threads are breakin'
And my back is achin';
Oh dear ah wish ah had wings.
Sometimes a shuttle flies out,
Gives some poor woman a clout,
There she lies bleeding
But nobody's heeding her;
Who's going to carry her out.
Tuner should tackle me loom,
'E'd rather sit on 'is bum,
'E's much too busy
A-courtin' our Lizzie,
'At ah cannot get 'im to come.
Lizzie is so easy led,
I think that 'e takes 'er to bed;
She always was skinny,
Now look at 'er pinny;
It's just abaht time they were wed.

folk-song sung by Thomas Sikes
Daniel (1899-1970) of Batley
by permission of A. E. Green and
the Director of The Institute of
Dialect and Folk Life Studies the
University of Leeds.

Wormald and Walker's Mill, Dewsbur

New Town, Queensbury Road, Halifax

"For twenty years," he said
on one occasion, "I was never
in bed at half-past five in
the morning."

Statement by Samuel Cunliffe
Lister quoted in the *Bradford
Observer,* Feb. 6th 1889 in an
article on Manningham Mills.

The Weaver to His Son

Be wary, be chary,
    Tak' head who tha courts.
Ther's lasses i' plenty,
    I' sahzes an' sorts;
Bud if tha s'be happy,
    Tak' on wi' a lass
'At's nimble wi' t'thimble
    An' careful wi't brass.

from *Rhymes in the North Country
    Humour* William Beaumont (published 1971)

112

Wood Terrace, Primrose Hill, Huddersfield

Huddersfield Road, Bailiff Bridge

Lees, Haworth

But he was a devout Methodist, for which (mistakenly, I think now) I rather despised him; and he was always trying to persuade me to take my Matric so that I too could become a teacher or a librarian. I couldn't bear the idea of teaching and though I liked the branch library at Engelsea with its smell of books and Pollywog paste and floor polish, I didn't like the rows of issue tickets behind the counter nor the stacks of membership forms, overdue notices, and the rest of it. The books were the thing and the machinery for issuing and recording them was another. Learning to write was one thing; studying for Matric was another. I knew even then that there wasn't much time and that there never would be. But Maurice meant well; he himself had found his vocation and he thought that I was in danger of missing mine.

from *The Queen of a Distant Country*
John Braine (published 1972)

Reuben had dark blue eyes, a mobile mouth, and a vague and wistful smile, which was strangely attractive and unexpected. His complexion was of a delicate tint, and he stooped a little. He was a clerk in an office.

"My son," his proud mother would say, "is a grand scholar, if you loike. Lord bless yer! he can add up in a breath loike greased lightnin', and wroite quick as t'express train."

She was inordinately proud of his attainments, and had an unbounded belief in his musical knowledge and literary successes; for could he not read music at sight, and had he not published verses in the Holgate Advertiser? and then, to crown all, was not he, Reuben, engaged to be married to his pretty cousin, Lillian Rathborne, of the Cross Keys down Pincheon Street? – to Lily, who was an only child, and had a voice like a lark and was that genteel that she taught in the Sunday Church school, and had lessons in French at one shilling and eightpence an hour.

from *Prose Idylls of the West Riding*
Lady Catherine Milnes Gaskell
(published 1907)

116

Cow and Calf Rocks, Ilkley

117

Pack-horse bridge, near Marsden

To all such *Wuthering Heights* must appear a rude and strange production. The wild moors of the north of England can for them have no interest; the language, the manners, the very dwellings and household customs of the scattered inhabitants of those districts, must be to such readers in a great measure unintelligible, and – where intelligible – repulsive. Men and women who, perhaps, naturally very calm, and with feelings moderate in degree, and little marked in kind, have been trained from their cradle to observe the utmost evenness of manner and guardedness of language, will hardly know what to make of this rough, strong utterance, the harshly manifested passions, the unbridled aversions, and head-long partialities of unlettered moorland hinds and rugged moorland squires who have grown up untaught and unchecked, except by mentors as harsh as themselves. A large class of readers, likewise, will suffer greatly from the introduction into the pages of this work of words printed with all their letters, which it has become the custom to represent by the initial and final letter only – a blank line filling the interval . . .

Haworth

Wuthering Heights was hewn in a wild workshop, with simple tools, out of homely materials. The statuary found a granite block on a solitary moor: gazing thereon, he saw how from the crag might be elicited a head, savage, swart, sinister; a form moulded with at least one element of grandeur – power. He wrought with a crude chisel, and from no model but the vision of his meditations. With time and labour, the crag took human shape; and there it stands colossal, dark, and frowning, half statue, half rock: in the former sense, terrible and goblin-like; in the latter, almost beautiful, for its colouring is of mellow grey, and the moorland moss clothes it; and heath, with its blooming bells and balmy fragrance, grows faithfully close to the giant's foot.

two excerpts from the preface by
Charlotte Brontë to the 1850 edition of
Wuthering Heights by Emily Brontë.

Keighley seen from Micklethwaite

Baildon Moor

Stainland, near Elland

As we sat 'neath the shady trees,
I on a stump, Nance on my knees,
Among the flowers, the birds, the
   bees,
Now, somehow, I felt ill at ease.

Says Nance, "What ails thee John?
   Is't fleas?"
Says I – But just then my ideas
Went nowhere, like a shower of
   peas,
Said I again, "Oh, Nancy Lees!"

Says she, " Oh John, you are a
   tease;"
Says I, "It's warm:" says she,
   "It ees;"
Says I once more, "Of all fair she's,
Thou are the fairest lass of Lees."

Says she, "Of all the fairest he's,
Thou art the rarest, Johnny Wees;"
Says I, "Thou'rt wine"; says she,
   "Thou'rt teas;"
Says I, "Thou'rt bread;" says she,
   "Thou'rt cheese.

So let's get wed, John if you please"
Says I, "Who'll pay the parson's
   fees,
For I've no brass – my breeches
   squeeze,
You'll find them empty to the
   knees."

I gave a sigh, she gave a squeeze,
And cried, "Begone from Nancy
   Lees,
For empty breeches will not please,
So off you go, you mouldy cheese."

"Johnny Wees and Nancy
Lees" by Henry Garrs of
Bradford, quoted in
Yorkshire Anthology,
J. Horshall Turner

Dockroyd, near Oakworth

Colne Road, near Stanbury

124

Eldwick, Bingley

Crosland Moor, Huddersfield

. . . the complete inventory of all the goods the last of the Cockcrofts left behind him:

Imprimis, long table in the house and a seat fixed behind it.

Item, 2 little chests in the little chamber, one a bad one but worth 18d.

Item, warping woah with a part of a pair of combs.

Item, one iron rong.

Item, bedstead in the little chamber with boards to make the bottom.

Item, 1 little foot chest.

Item, 6 old chairs made of spelted only one made of throwne (i.e. turned on a laithe) worth 5s.

(Warping woah: probably same as "warping woose" or "warping wouthe" – the machine in which threads are arranged into warps and thus made ready for weaving.)

from an article "The Manor of Harden" in the *Bradford Antiquary* 1938, Clifford Whone.

Oud Betty's Advice

So Mary, lass, tha'rt bahn to wed
I't morning wi' young blacksmith Ned,
And tho it makes thy mother sad,
    It's like to be;
I've nout ageean yond decent lad
    No more ner thee.

But let me tell thee what ta due,
For my advice might help thee thru;
Be kind, and to thy husband true,
    An I'll be bun
Tha'll nivver hev a day ta rue,
    For out tha's done.

Nah, try to keep thi former knack,
And due thi weshing in a crack,
Bud don't be flaid to bend thi back,
    Tha'll nobbut sweeat;
So try an hev a bit o'tack,
    An do it neat.

Be sure tha keeps fra being a flirt,
An pride thysel e being alert, –
An mind to mend thi husband's shirt,
    An keep it clean;
It wod thy poor oud mother hurt,
    If tha wor mean.

Don't kal abaht like monny a wun,
Then hev to broil, an sweeat, an run;
Bud alus hev thy dinner done,
    Withaht a mooild;
If its nobbut meil, lass, set it on,
    An hev it boiled.

from Random Rhymes and Rambles
Bill o'th'Hoylus End
(William Wright)
(published 1876)

So Mary, I've no more to say –
Tha gets thy choice an' tak thy way:
An if tha leets to rue, I pray,
    Don't blame thy mother:
I wish you monny a happy day
    We wun another.

Skipton Parish Church

My Gronfathur's Grave

Nut a puff stirred a leaf o' them grand owd trees,
    'At owershadded the grahnd ov ahr village church,
As I gloared wi' full een on a gerse-grown heap,
    Under t'shade of a knotted an' time-worn birch.

T'owd tree, like a priest in his hoaly robes,
    Stude solemn an' grey anent t'western dlow,
An' liftin' its arms into t'silent air,
    Seemed to pray for t'poar fellah 'at slept below.

from *Dialect and Other Poems*
    Ben Preston (published 1881)
    (opening verses of the poem)

Thornton Parish Church, near Skipton

Ilkley Moor

The Poacher's Song

Come all ye brethren of the night,
    Who rang the mountain, wood
      and vale,
And in the moonshine chase
  delight,
    May our true friendship never
      fail!
Then drink around, your cares
  confound,
    Ye champions of the wire;
The field, the moor, will we range
  o'er,
    Nor care for lord nor squire.

The parliament, such youths as we,
    With laws may strive to bind;
But they as soon in cords might tie
    The lightenings or the wind!
By Cynthia's beams we cross the
  streams,
    To fetch the game away;
Then here we rest, with bumpers
  blest,
    And banish fear away.

The lord upon the hunting day
    Such pleasures never knew,
When Echo bore the sounds away,
    The hounds – the fox in view;
As when the hares are caught in
  pairs,
    Upon the glittering frost!
Should we be fined, what need we
  mind,
    Since others pay the cost?

So long as planets rise and set,
    Or timorous hares can run,
The Poacher true will hang his net,
    And level sure his gun;
The high park wall, spring guns and
  all,
    And keepers strong with beer,
We value not, nor shun the spot,
    If hares are frisking there.

We stop not at the rivers deep,
    The frost or winter's snow;
The lazy keepers soundly sleep,
    When tempest wildly blow.
Of rain and hail let Jove's great pail
    Be emptied from on high;
The darker night the more delight,
    The greater numbers die.

from A collection of poems
John Nicholson
(published 1844)

Winterburn, near Skipton

'The Weaver'

Ther's t'meyt hung dahn afore t'fire ta rooast,
Ther's t'puddin' on t'brandree afore it ta tooast,
Potates top o' t'hop, they'll be done enif sooin,
But Ah think tha can weive a few more bobbins bi nooin.

attributed to John Bramley of Bramley
from *White Rose Garland*
(published 1949)

132

Farm at Sparkenhouse Lane, near Sowerby village

Outlane, Huddersfield

February 1568   Richard Hyrste, of Mylner Brygge, commynge from Halifax
Market, on Satyrdaye xij day of Februarie, was through a greate snow left
and stopped – the dryfte of snow was so very great, and beynge alone all
Satyrdaye nyghte, peryshed and died on Linlaye Moore, not farre from a cross
called Hayghe Crosse, and was found on the morrow after, his horse
standynge bye him, *even harde* by hym, and was brought home to his own
house, and buried at Almondburye, Monday ye xiiij daye of Februarie – and
Elizabeth, the daughter of George Harpyn, an infant, with him.

extract from The Parish Church Register, Almondbury

134

Colne Valley, Huddersfield

It was pleasant, after his long weeks in the saddle, to feel the springy moor grass under his feet; it would be pleasanter still, he told himself, to stretch his limbs on his own lang settle and drink a well-earned measure from the loving-cup which stood above the mantel. And there would be time for all that before returning to Jessie – need of it, too, belike, should his cousin be moved to sharpen her wit at his expense. A score of kindly thoughts crowded to Kit's mind as he came in sight of Withens; he let his eye fall tenderly on the old home, the old queer splashes of green that lay within the grim hand of the moor. The green intaken land was there, as he had known it; but in place of the remembered chimney-stack and gables and clustered outbuildings, only roofless piles of blackened stonework reared themselves. He rubbed his eyes, as if doubtful whether sleep had followed his hard cross-country ride; but a second glance at the ruins convinced him that the Master of Withens was homeless. He remembered the Carlesses, forgotten until now in the warm outgoing of his heart towards the thought of home; and he knew that none but they could have done this thing.

For a long while he stood there, looking down stupidly on the homestead. Then, on the sudden, something flashed into his eyes and into the grim curves of mouth and jaw. He made forward steadily, until he stood facing the cracked walls; he glanced from side to side – saw the black squares which showed where latterly his ricks of straw and hay had stood – marked the drear look of the mistals wherein his cattle had lately fidgeted on their chains. The first inrush of grief was silenced; he nodded gravely at the ruins, as if they were ghosts that had stayed to ask for vengeance.

from *Ricroft of Withens*
Halliwell Sutcliffe (published 1898)

136

East Riddlesden Hall, near Keighley

After playing lady's maid to the new comer, and putting my cakes in the oven, and making the house and kitchen cheerful with great fires, befitting Christmas eve, I prepared to sit down and amuse myself by singing carols, all alone; regardless of Joseph's affirmations that he considered the merry tunes I chose as next door to songs. He had retired to private prayer in his chamber, and Mr. and Mrs. Earnshaw were engaging Missy's attention by sundry gay trifles brought for her to present to the little Lintons, as an acknowledgement of their kindness. They had invited them to spend the morrow at Wuthering Heights, and the invitation had been accepted, on one condition: Mrs. Linton begged that her darlings might be kept carefully apart from that "naughty swearing boy".

Under these circumstances I remained solitary. I smelt the rich scent of the heating spices: and admired the shining kitchen utensils, the polished clock, decked with holly, the silver mugs ranged on a tray ready to be filled with mulled ale for supper; and above all, the speckless purity of my particular care – the scoured and well-swept floor . . .

from *Wuthering Heights*
Emily Brontë (published 1847)

137

Lower Old Hall, Norland Town, near Sowerby Bridge

East Riddlesden Hall

All round the lands held by the farmer who lives in the remains of Howley Hall are stone houses of to-day, occupied by the people who are making their living and their fortunes by the woollen mills that encroach upon and shoulder out the proprietors of ancient halls. These are to be seen in every direction, picturesque, many gabled, with heavy stone carvings of coats of arms for heraldic ornament; belonging to decayed families, from whose ancestral lands field after field had been shorn away, by the urgency of rich manufacturers pressing hard upon necessity.

A smoky atmosphere surrounds these old dwellings of former Yorkshire squires, and blights and blackens the ancient trees that overshadow them; cinder paths lead to them; the ground round about is sold for building upon; but still the neighbours, though they subsist by a different state of things, remember that their forefathers lived in agricultural dependence upon the owners of these halls; and treasure up the traditions connected with the stately households that existed centuries ago . . .

from *Life of Charlotte Brontë*
Mrs. Gaskell (published 1857)

Norland Hall, near Sowerby Bridge

Old Hall, East Ardsley, near Wakefield

Vita Uxoris Honestae

To live at home in howswyverie
To order well my famyle
To see they lyve not idillye
To brynge up children vertuislye
To relyeve poor foulk willinglye
This is my care with modestye
To lead my lyfe in honestye.

To bragge or to boast of noble
    parentage
To the ys none honour of yt live
    amysse
Then serve we God duly in every
    age
Not willing our own will but fyrst
    willynge his
Obeying our howsbands in what
    lawful is
Who howswifely taketh
    delightyng in this
Well may be called good matron
    or maistris.

from the genealogical paintings at
Woodsome Hall, Huddersfield
(Sir John Kay's family 1573)

Near Kirkheaton, Huddersfield

Mount Tabor Methodist Church, near Halifax

Pitt Hill, Trooper Lane, Halifax

To limit the hours of factory toil
He stood undaunted 'midst the broil
Of those who strove the work to foil
    Of the king of the factory children.
But infant's labour was assailed,
And petty tyrants writhed and wailed,
With oaths and curses they assailed,
    The king of the factory children.
But gratitude the chain has brike,
Which bound him to the tyrant's yoke,
The prison house no more's the walk
    Of the king of the factory children.

> one of four verses from a broadside
> *Oastler the Factory King*
> (printed in Halifax 1844)

Just let me tell you my little "pets", in passing; it's just as I said it would be; the Factory Bill given by Lord Althorpe, at the request of the Masters – the "Eight Hours – the "Two Sets" – the "Education"(!) Bill, which makes *you* have to pay for your "Certificates", is now found *not to act* – even so as to please its makers! I knew it never would, it never could: and I have told the Public so many times. I'll tell you a "bit of a secret". I was in London a few weeks ago, and I saw Lord Ashley; he is still your friend – and we had a little chat about you children: and he said something to Lord Althorpe about the Bill the latter thrust upon us; you will, I dare say, want to know what the two Lords said about it; but for once I'll copy a very bad precedent – I'll say as Brougham did to the Lords, "*now, that is the only thing which I will not tell you.*" But you have heard there has been a rare stir among the "Factory Commissioners". They were going to sleep till then; but *now* they are sickening the masters with a vengeance – and the masters *want* Lord Ashley to have an "ELEVEN HOURS" bill; but his Lordship loves you too well for that; and so does SADLER and BULL and WOOD and CONDY: and I do too my little Pets. After all "WE WILL HAVE THE TEN HOUR BILL" won't we? never mind BAINES, he wants we all know, to work you *Eleven Hours* but the Doctors say you cannot stand it.

> from a letter by Richard Oastler in a pamphlet
> *The Argus and Demagogue*
> (Huddersfield 1834)

West End Mills, Dewsbury

Armitage Street, Primrose Hill, Huddersfield

Denholme

Tell tale tit

Your tongue shall split

And every little dog

Shall have a little bit.

See all, hear all, say nowt;

Eat all, sup all, pay nowt;

And if tha ivver does owt for nowt

Do it for thisen.

Rhymes heard by the author as a child

147

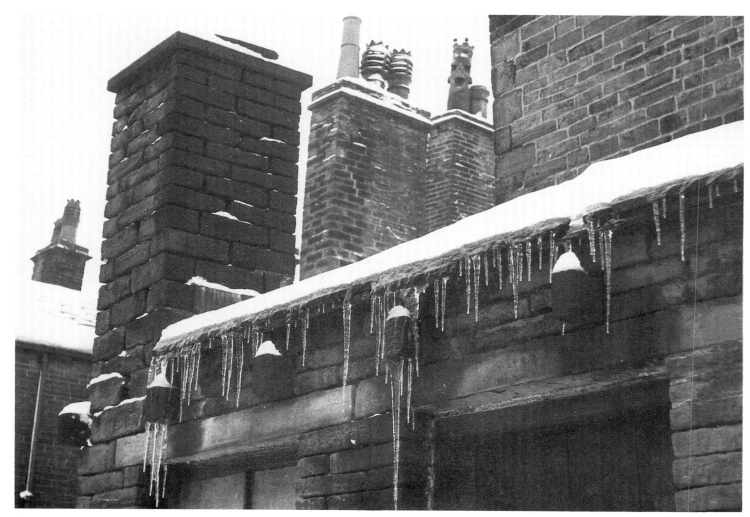

Spring Garden Street, Queensbury

I was in a certain house on baking day, where the wife gave a pinch of dough to her little lass to play with; but I came away, for I could not thoil to see good dough wasted. I thought then that in these days folk hardly know they are living –. When I was a little lad I found a penny once. There were seven of us lads in the family, and we took daily turns at scraping the porridge pan. I went to my father and told him about this penny, and said I would give it him if I might scrape the pan three times running. And that way I would have wared (spent) it. We had nought but "porridge and stop" then, and sometimes we had not that. I can tell of my mother fainting one morning when she had served us all round and left herself none; and that morning I had scraped the pan.

from *The Web of an Old Weaver*
J. Keighley Snowden (published 1896)

"Aw've heeard mi fayther tell ' at when he wor a lad, ther wor a family o' five on 'em, an' they all worked at th'factory, an' as lads will, they sometimes stopt aat soa lat ov a neet 'at they fun it varry hard to get up next morning; an' they had to be up at five o'clock 'cos they'd a long way to walk. Nah, mi gronfayther could nawther get up nor call aat, but ha do yo think he managed to get 'em 'aat o'bed? He used to allus keep abaat a barro looad o' brokken bricks at his bedside, an' th'lads used to know as sooin as they felt 'em flying abaat their heeads 'at it wor time to be stirrin: one used to be enuff in a general way, but th'second wor sure to do it, even if he wor a hard sleeper, an' if th'third didn't wakken him, you could book him for a tombstooan ony minit. Nah that's what aw call technical eddication."

from *Yorkshire Puddin'*
John Hartley (published 1877)
the chapter "Th'New School Board"

St. Andrew's Junior School, Brighouse

I just want to reyk up a toathree recolleckshuns of hah we us'td to spend Crismas when I wor a lad, an' that worrent yesterday. Befoar dewin' so, I can't help thinkin' 'at t'guid owd Crismas time is'nt as mitch thowt on nah as it us'td to be. What wi' Bank Holidays, cheap trips, an' sitch like things, times hes altered a lot sin' I wor a lad, bud I'm noan bahn to say for't better. At onnyrate, gi'me t'owd feshuned way o' celebratin' Crismas, if ye pleeas.

For one thing, I don't think t'owd Crismas custom ov goin' to see yer relashuns is hauf so mitch thowt on as it us'td to be. Ay dear! what a spuffle ther wor at ahr hahse when mi Ont Hannah an' their Sam (that wor mi unkel) cam tut t'dinner a Crismas Day, an' browt three o' t'yungsters wi' 'em. I'st nivver forget them dooments as long as I liv'. T'day befoar Crismas mi mother wor as fierce as a buck-ferrit, fettlin' up, an' bakin', an' gettin' all reddy for t'next day so as nut to be dun dahn bi' mi Ont Hannah. So ye see ther's a bit o' pride left i' t'family yet.

We wor nobbud workin' fowk, but mi mother prided hersen on hevin' a few things belongin' to her forelders, an' ameng 'em wor a set o' pewter plates, two quart jugs, an' a real silver teahpot. Besides these, we had six brass cannel sticks, two pairs o' snuffers, an' t'owd family warmin' pan. These things wor seldom ivver used, except t'company teahpot, bud they wor all kept as breet as a new pin, an' hed an extra rubbin' just befoar t'Tide Sunday an' Crismas Day. T'day befoar Crismas shoo'd t'plum puddin' to get reddy, beside a lot ov other things, so us yungsters wor packed off to bed i' gooid time, agean wor likin', for we wanted to stop up an' hear t'chappil singers 'at allus cam' to let Crismas on t'next doar.

from Yorkshire Speyks
William Cudworth (published 1906)
from the chapter "Owd Crismas Time"

And as the snow drifted high on the moorland and came whirling down in soft flakes to the valley below, until at last every roof in Ludenstall was thick and whitened and all the streets were touched with Northern magic; as they raised their glasses and joined hands and sang in chorus, and bells that seemed as old and mysterious as the flying and featured night itself rang out the Old, rang in the New – the last letter of all was being carried through a black and dripping railway cutting in the hills, to be slung with a thousand others on board a liner that would soon go hooting through the dark to Canada;

My Dear Daughter: I am writing these lines to say I am still in the pink and hoping you are the same. We are now in Good Old Yorks, and so had a good and merry Xmas. I had my Xmas dinner with Landlady and Family and had a goose and pudding and etc. I wish you had been there Lily, to keep your old Father company. I went on tram to Bruddersford and called at 51. Your Mother was looking poorly but when I asked her said she was alright and as she was a bit short with me could get nothing out of her. Albert is still there but did not see him and was glad not to but I saw our Leonard who is doing well. Your Mother told me you had not written to her only to me so I think Lily you had better write to her as well sometime for she is your Mother when all is said and done and as I say is looking poorly. The Good Comps. are going well here and will do so, if I know any thing, at other places on the road. Wishing you and Jack a Happy New Year and all the best. Keep on writing to me at 51 and they will send on. And keep your heart up Lily we will have a good laugh the two of us yet together.
With love and kisses,

> from yr Father
> J. Oakroyd

from *The Good Companions*
  J. B. Priestley (published 1929)

1755   In this year the act of parliament . . . . was passed, entitled "an act for enlighting the streets and lanes of Leeds". The preamble of this act is as follows:– 'Whereas the town of Leeds, in the County of York, is a place of great trade and large extent, consisting of many streets, narrow lanes and alleys, inhabited by great numbers of tradesmen, manufacturers, artificers, and others, who in the prosecution of and carrying out of their respective trades and manufactures, are obliged to pass and repass through the same as well in the night as in the day time: and whereas several burglaries, robberies and other outrages and disorders have lately been committed, and many more attempted within the said town &c, and the enlightening of the said streets and lanes and regulating the pavements thereof would be of great advantage, and tend not only to the security and preservation of the person and properties of the said inhabitants of the town, but to the benefit and convenience of strangers, and persons resorting to the several markets within the said town &c".

The first streets which were lighted under this act were Cross-parish and New-street – so called because it was the first place in Leeds upon which the word street was imposed. The system of lighting was by means of oil lamps which were used for 28 years after, when a gas company was incorporated by act of parliament.

from *Annals and History of Leeds*
compiled by John Mayhall (1860)

Meanwood Road, Leeds

Bilton Place, City Road, Bradford

Back Chapel Street, Leeds Road, Bradford

When I were at 'ome wi' me feyther
  an' me mother,
I never 'ad no fun,
An' they kept me at it fra' morn till
  neet,
So I thought fra' them I'd run.
Leeds fair were comin' on,
An' I thought I'd 'ave a spree,
So I clapp'd on me Sunday coat an'
  'at,
An' went right merrily.
    With a rumpsy bumpsy bay,
    Ri-too-loo-da-laddie;
    Rumpsy bumpsy day,
    Ri-too-loo-da-laddie.
First thing I saw were a great big
  mill,
I'd never seen yon afore;
There were winnies an' jennies an'
  slubbers an' spinners,
An' wheels by mony a score;
An' every strap it had a wheel,
An' every wheel a strap,
"By gum!" says I to t'maister man.
"Owd Harry's a rare strong chap."
    With a rumpsy bumpsy bay,
    etc.

Next thing I saw were Leeds 'Owd
  Church,
I'd nobbt been i' yon i' me days,
An' I almost felt ashamed of misen,
For I didn't know their ways.
There were twenty or thirty folk
I' tubs an' boxes sat,
When up there comes a saucy owd
  chap—
Says he, "Lad tak' off thi 'at."
    With a rumpsy bumpsy bay
      etc.
An' then there cam' a great Lord
  Mayor,
An o'er his shoulder a club,
An' he donned on a white sack
  poke,
An' gat into t'top-most tub.
An then there cam' another chap,
An' I think they called him Ned,
An' he gat into t'bottom-most tub,
An' mocked what t'other chap said.
    With a rumpsy bumpsy bay,
      etc.

An' then they began to pray and
    preach,
They prayed for George our King,
When up jumps t'chap in t'top-
    most tub,
Says he "Good folks let's sing."
An' I thought some sang very well,
While others did grunt an' groan,
An' everyone sang what they liked,
So I sang 'Bob and Joan'.
    With a rumpsy bumpsy day,
        etc.

An' when t'praying an' preaching
    were over,
An' folks were going away,
I went to t'chap in t'bottom-most
    tub,
Says I, "Lad, what's to pay?"
"Why nowt, me lad," says he,
By gum I were right fane,
So I cleaved hold of me owd club-
    stick,
An' went whistling out again.
    With a rumpsy bumpsy day,
        etc.

a folk-song collated by the Institute of Dialect and
Folk-life Studies, The University, Leeds:
this version given by Mrs. G. Carney of Wombwell

Leeds Parish Church

Wormald's Yard, Leeds

Wharfe.   Hold! If the sources of Aire are veiled in mystery, and his middle shrouded in a smoke-screen, he is hardly to blame for that. There are black spots on the sun, and even Ouse is not entirely undefiled. In one sense, surely, it is a compliment to Aire that men have so crowded his banks and that great cities jostle for his possession. If there are no Abbots and no fat monks in his dale, at least there are some fat Alderman and Councillors; if no flocks of sheep in his cities, at least there are the droves of hogs. – And if Kirkstall is now a soot-scarred skeleton, at least there is the Post Office, Boar Lane, Swinegate, the Town Hall and the Sewage Works. Progress, we are assured, is making great strides; and certainly many of the mill chimneys that cast their canopy over the West Riding are taller than Kirkstall's towers. If Aire has lost his cows and his pigs, certainly he has any number of barges, brimful of coal and pig-iron.

from *Boon Fellows* by Alfred Brown (published 1928)

Canal and River Aire from the viaduct, Armley, Leeds

Wolseley View, Burley, Leeds

Bradford for cash,
Halifax for dash,
Wakefield for pride and poverty;
Huddersfield for show,
Sheffield what's low,
Leeds for dirt and vulgarity.

from *English Folk-Lore*
A. R. Wright (published 1928)

By 1875 there were over 130 societies in existence in Yorkshire, of which 120 were in the West Riding. Of these, only six had a continuous history before 1840, including the oldest of all, Meltham Mills. The Co-op had become part of the way of life of working people. Some co-ops – like Greenfield – provided houses at low rents for their members. Others ran funeral parlours, taking over the functions of the old burial clubs. Some had libraries – as at Batley – and many invested their surplus funds in the manufacturing associations of the Co-operative Production Societies. All had one thing in common – they were retail societies which paid a dividend on purchases . . .

The "divi", which was usually declared twice a year, paid for holidays, Christmas presents and so on, and provided a cushion for the hard-pressed housewife when times were difficult during strikes and lock-outs or when domestic tragedies struck the family . . .

The co-op may not have blazed a trail leading to the Owenite utopia, but it did a great deal, in the spirit of Victorian self-help, to make everyday life in industrial Yorkshire more tolerable for hundreds and thousands of working folks. It also fed the spirit of self-reliant working class dignity which was a striking feature of the late Victorian era.

from *Industrial Revolution in Yorkshire*
Fred Singleton (published 1970)

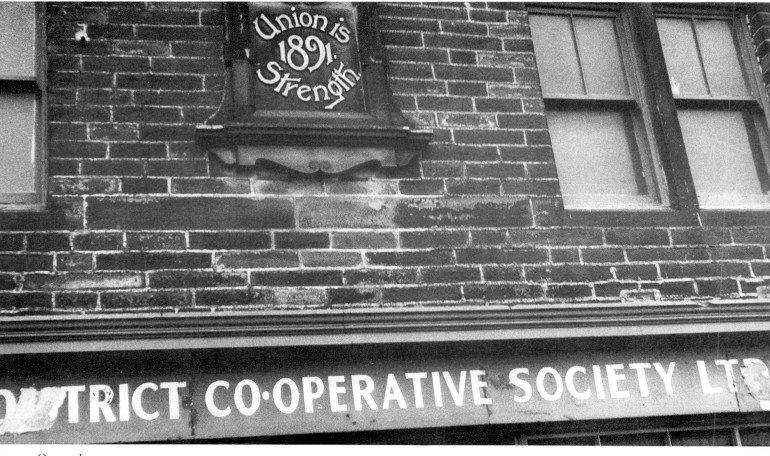

Queensbury

There's a shop called the Co-op in the High Street,
By Gum it's a great idea;
For out of what you spend, you get a dividend
Three times ev'ry year.
When Ma takes two shillings for her share,
She shouts feeling like a millionaire:–

Chorus

"Stop and shop at the 'Cwop', the Co-op shop,
What a shop is the 'cwop' the Co-op shop!
You can buy from a chop to a prop or a mop,
Or a bottle o' ginger pop at the 'Cwop' shop.
As the Pop-shop is next to the 'Cwop' shop,
When you've done your popping in the Pop-shop,
You hop out of the Pop-shop and pop into the 'Cwop' shop,
A proper shop to shop at is the 'Cwop' shop!"

1st verse and Chorus of the song *Stop and shop
at the Co-op Shop*, sung by Gracie Fields,
(written in 1929) R. P. Weston and Bert Lee

Stanbury, near Haworth ›

Knaresborough

"There's nowt like Bridlington sands," he would say in self defence. "I'm noan sayin' but there's a better colour i' t'watter at Blackpool, but what there's ower mich wind on t'sea. Sea-watter gits into your mouth when you're swimmin' and then you've to blow like a grampus. Scarborough's ower classy for t'likes o' Mary an' me; it's all reight for betterny-bodies that likes to dizen theirselves out an' sook cigars on church parade. But me an't'owd lass allus go te Bridlington. It's homely, is Bridlington, an' you're not runnin' up ivvery minute ageean foreign counts an' countesses that ought to bide whear they belang, an' keep theirsens to theirsens."

from *Tales of the Ridings*
F. W. Moorman (published 1920)
the chapter "The Inner Voice"

Ode to Summer

O! welcome lovely summer,
  With thi golden days so long,
When the throstle and the
  blackbird
    So charm us wi' their song;
When the lark in early morning
  Takes his aerial flight;
An' the humming bat an'
  buzzard
    Frolic in the night.

O! welcome, lovely summer,
  With her rainbow's lovely
    form;
Her thunner an' her leetnin,
  An' her grandeur in the storm:
With her sunshine an' her
  shower,
    And her wurlin of the dust;
An' the maiden with her flagon,
  To sleck the mower's thirst.

O! welcome, lovely summer,
  When the woods wi' music
    ring;
And the bees so heavy laden,
  To their hives their treasures
    bring:
When we seek some shady
  bower,
    Or some lovely little dell,
Or bivock in the sunshine,
  Besides some cooling well.

O! welcome, lovely summer,
  With her roses in full bloom;
When the cowslaps an' the
  lalack
    Deck the cottage home:
When the cherry an' the berry
  Gives a grandeur to the
    charm:
And the clover and the haycocks
  Scent the little farm.

O! welcome, lovely summer,
  With the partridge on the
    wing;
When the tewit an' the
  moorgame,
    Up fra the heather spring,
From the crowbar an' the
  billber,
    An' the bracken an' the ween;
As from the noisy tadpole,
  We hear the crackin din.
    O! welcome, lovely summer.

from *Random Rhymes and Rambles*
  Bill o'th'Hoylus End (William Wright)
  (published 1876)

Barnoldswick

In summer, too, there was the joy of cricket. Sometimes when the weather was fine and Mr. Shaw in an expansive mood, he would allow his traveller and his works manager an afternoon off together to watch Yorkshire playing some other county (inferior of course in their opinion) at Bradford. The train ambled through the winding green valleys and puffed up sombre hills and stopped at the special cricket-ground station, which confirmed its identity by a painted decoration of bat and wickets, and a red ball far too big in proportion. Then the indolent lounging hours on the open wooden benches, the white-flannelled figures on the pitch with famous names, the delicious 'chock' of the bat on ball, the graceful swift athletic action, the excitement of the mounting score competing with the flying minutes, the long, long discussions of famous innings, of slow-bowlers' hat tricks, of difficult umpires' decisions. Winnie made them sandwiches for lunch and sometimes accompanied them, looking fresh and summery in a thin frock of mauve-figured voile and a large white hat; but Winnie found cricket rather slow and was apt to make audible mordant comments on the batsmen which embarrassed her brother and Morcar.

from *The Rise of Henry Morcar*
Phyllis Bentley (published 1946)

Cricket ground, Beckfoot, Bingley

Although the industrial revolution in the nineteenth century besmirched many fair tracts of Britain, by no means all the mills erected during that period lacked architectural merit. Indeed, some mill-owners spent substantial sums on embellishing the bond between utilitarian needs and aesthetic appearance.

Typical of such thought for the public weal is the 755 foot stack dominating the Manningham (Bradford) factory founded by Samuel Cuncliffe Lister, later Lord Masham. The name "Lister's Pride" was given to the structure officially in 1873 when he ascended the chimney and took part in a christening ceremony at the top.

from *It's Odd, It's Yorkshire*
Arthur Gaunt
(published 1971)

Near Luddenden Foot

Mill Street, Low Moor, Bradford

Aw think aw nivver saw a moor miserable seet i' mi life! Th' big empty fire grate, lukkin bi th'leet ov a tallow cannel like th'entrance to some place at aw hooap we shall nivver see, – th'sweep wor one o' th'blackest an' ugliest ov his tribe, an' he wor reared ageean th'table smokin' a short pipe as black as hissen; an' th'childer wor unweshed, an' peeark'd up i'th'winder bottom aght o'th'gate, thrang lickin' th'traikle off three shives o'looaf, an' ommost flaid aght o'ther wit an hawf starved to deeath, – an' Ameely lukkin, – well, awl say nowt abaat her luks, – but if shoo'd lukt like that once on a time awst ha' been a single chap yet. Ee, gow! but it wor cold that morning! Aw dooant believe i'takkin owt varry strong befoor th'braikfast, but if ther'd been a drop o'summat short i'th'hasse aw believe awst ha' brokken teetotal that morning'.

"Well", aw sed, turnin' to th'sweep, "arn't ta baan to mak a begginin?"

from *The Clock Almanack for 1880*
John Hartley
(the article entitled "Sweep! oh! Sweep!!")

Hipperholme

Primrose Hill, Huddersfield

"But here's the other side – the spiritual side. You've allus been a good-living woman, one of the main folks at the chappill, and a reggler attender at the class and the prayer meetings, and you're the last I should have thought would have given way to this new-fangled notion of pride and conceit that a body can't wash themselves without having a room specially set apart for the job . . .

Now I haven't had my head washed for fotty years, and if it pleases the Lord to spare me, I shan't have it washed for another ten. I keeps meself as clean as one here and there, and I does it with humility in a wash-basin with a flannel, in me own bedroom with the blind pulled down – not stark naked in a great bath in which a body might easily be drowned if they took a fit or fell dizzy or owt of that there . . .

I knows our Sairy Jane, when she got wed and went to live in the town, had a house with a bathroom in it, and at first she was capped with it till they were all coughing one again another and never had a doctor off the doorstep. Then she said, 'No more roaring coals away under that boiler and bubbling and shaking of pipes and cisterns to scare me out of my wits and fetch one cold on top of another!' I think after that they contented with washing themselves well."

from *Humours of Village Life*
J. Fairfax-Blakeborough (published 1932)
the chapter "About Baths and Bathrooms"

ASS – Ashes. "Ass-pan" – a tin box or pan placed beneath the fire-grate to receive the ashes as they fall down. "Ther'assing t'roading an't corser!" – sprinkling the road and causeway with ashes, as in frosty weather.

ASS – Ask. Ah ast him to gi'e muh't an' he wodn't". "Ass him agean then, ther's nowt to be gotten wi'art assing.

from the glossary in
Yorkshire Notes and Queries
Edited by Forshaw (Bradford 1909)

Reservoir, Wessenden Valley

The puddle bank next gave way; and then, shortly after midnight, as if a thunderbolt had pierced the immense wall, the whole mass of earthwork constituting the inner embankment rolled over with a crash that reverberated like the boom of death far down the moonlit valley, and instantly the pent-up waters which had formed this gigantic reservoir rushed in one mighty and devastating flood into the sleeping valley below . . .

Desolation and death overspread the Holme valley for miles; mills were swept down, trees were uprooted, steam-engines' boilers were carried away; and among the struggling masses of wreck the moonlight revealed bags of wool, carding machines, dye-pans, looms, furniture . . .

from *Yorkshire Stories Retold*
James Burnley (published 1885)
an account of the Holme Valley disaster of 1852

177

Sowerby Croft

This business is the clothing trade, for the convenience of which the houses are thus scattered and spread upon the sides of the hills, as above, even from the bottom to the top; the reason is this; such has been the bounty of nature to this otherwise frightful country, that two things essential to the business, as well as to the ease of the people are found here, and that in a situation which I never saw the like of in any part of England; and I believe, the like is not to be seen so contrived in any part of the world; I mean coals and running water upon the tops of the highest hills. This seems to have been directed by the wise hand of Providence for the very purpose which is now served by it, namely, the manufactures, which otherwise could not be carried on; neither indeed could one fifth of the inhabitants be supported without them, for the land could not maintain them. After we had mounted the third hill, we found the country, in short, one continued village, tho' mountainous every way as before; hardly a house standing out of speaking distance from one another, and (which soon told us their business) the day clearing up, and the sun shining, (the sun reflecting its rays) to us, I thought it was the most agreable sight that I ever saw, for the hills, as I say, rising and falling so thick, and the valleys opening sometimes one way, sometimes another, so that sometimes we could see two or three miles this way, sometimes as far another; sometimes like the streets near St. Giles, called the Seven Dials; we could see through the glades almost every way around us, yet look which way we would, high to the tops and low to the bottom, it was all the same; innumerable houses and tenters, and a white piece upon every tenter.

But to return to the reason of dispersing the houses, as above; I found, as our road pass'd among them, for indeed no road could do otherwise, wherever we pass'd any house we found a little rill or gutter of running water, if the house was above the road, it came from it, and cross'd the way to run to another; if the house was below us, it cross'd us from some other distant house above it, and at every considerable house was a manufactory or work-house, and as they could not do this business without water, the little streams were so parted and guided by gutters or pipes, and by turning and dividing the streams, that none of those houses were without a river, if I may call it so, running into and through their work-houses.

from *Tour through the Whole Island of Great Britain*
Daniel Defoe (published 1724-1727)

Wheer 'as ta bin sin' ah saw thee?
    On Ilkley Moor baht 'at.

Tha's been a coortin' Mary Jane,
    On Ilkley Moor baht 'at.

Tha'll go and get thi deeath o' cowd,
    On Ilkley Moor baht 'at.

Then we shall 'a'ta bury thee,
    On Ilkley Moor baht 'at.

Then t'worms'll come an' eit thee up,
    On Ilkley Moor baht 'at.

Then t'ducks'll come an' eit up
  worms,
    On Ilkley Moor baht 'at.

Then we shall come an' eit up t'ducks,
    On Ilkley Moor baht 'at.

Then we shall all 'ave etten thee,
    On Ilkley Moor baht 'at.

Traditional West Riding song.

The Swastika Stone (Bronze Age), Ilkley Moor

180

When I'm ower thrang wi' wark on a washin'-day I just set misen down on t'chair and think o't'rest o'heaven, an' I say ower to misen yon lines that I larnt frae my mother:

'I knew a poor lass that allus were tired,
Shoo lived in a house wheer help wasn't hired.
Her last words on earth were, "Dear friends, I am going'
Wheer weshin' aint' doon, nor sweepin', nor sewin'.
Don't weep for me now, don't weep for me niver,
I'm boun' to do nowt for iver an' iver."'

from *Tales of the Ridings*
F. W. Moorman (published 1920)
the chapter "The Inner Voice"

Warley, near Halifax

Dick Hudson's stands high above Eldwick village and is on the moor edge running from Bingley in Middle Airedale to Otley, the market town in Wharfedale . . .

. . . the inn reached its zenith in the not so distant days when walking over the moors from Shipley or Baildon was popular. At Easter and Whitsuntide hundreds of city workers slogged along the moorland track after having regaled themselves at Dick Hudson's, this being the last place where they could fortify themselves before they reached the end of their trek at the Wharfedale spa.

In readiness for the invasion by the army of hikers, already hungry after their preliminary stage of the hike, the inn larders were crammed with enormous piles of home-made bread, buns, cakes and tarts. There were huge stacks of sliced ham and bucketfuls of eggs ready to be placed in a great frying pan more than 18″ across. The sizzling and appetizing aroma were part of the enjoyment experienced by the continuous stream of walkers who flocked to Dick Hudson's at holiday time.

from *It's Odd – It's Yorkshire*
Arthur Gaunt (published 1971)

Near Eldwick, Bingley

Dick Hudson's, Eldwick, Bingley

The River Aire, Bingley

The graveyard, Haworth Parsonage

Huddersfield Town Hall

"Every member in rotation as they stand on the list shall have the privilege of selecting the Oratorio to be performed at the next meeting, providing that a majority of the members think that copies can be procured. On the regular monthly meetings the band shall play not more than four instrumental pieces."

"On the monthly nights any member shall be allowed to give his opinion after the performance of any piece of music, providing he do so in a respectable, friendly and becoming manner, but no one shall be allowed to stop, interrupt or make any disturbance on the orchestra during the performance of any piece of music on pain of forfeiting the sum of *two shillings and sixpence* for every such offence or be excluded."

"Any member being intoxicated or using obscene language or calling any other member or members *bye-names* at any of the meetings shall forfeit sixpence for each offence."

> from the rules laid down at the inception of the
> Huddersfield Choral Society (1836)

186

December 1933 (8½ years old)

Yesterday it was Sunday after Christmas day and we all went to chapel with pa. Micklethwaite is a long way off and ma was grumbling about the tram journey and the long walk up the hill to get there. First of all we went to Grandma Whone's for tea at 5, John Street, Crossflatts. The best tea service was out, a beautiful tea-pot made of silver on a stand and special cups and saucers, and lace mats. We had ham sandwiches, very small and thin with mustard, peaches and cream, and Christmas cake so thick with fruit and so hard I could hardly bite it. Afterwards we walked to Micklethwaite.

When we went into the chapel,* toys brought for poor children were spread around the pulpit. We could hardly find a place, so we were squashed in at the end of a pew. First the caretaker came up from the basement with a long gas-lighter to light the lamps on the walls. Once or twice he had to pull the chain that alters the pressure to get them to light. The last lamps to be lit were behind the choir seats and the very last was behind the pulpit. I like that part of the service – the gas has a gentle hiss and everybody is settling down. Next, Joe Rennard, my god-father got up from the front and went to the harmonium where, after a lot of pedalling the music started up. Soon after, the choir came up the stairs from the basement, one by one, the women first. There was Mrs. Joul, Mrs. Myers, Annie Preston, Janey Preston, and some others. The men came after – Herbert Robershaw, Bob Shaw, Herbert Preston, Harry Preston, Stanley Myers, my pa and some others. Finally the preacher came up. He announced the first hymn. It was Christians Awake. I have never heard such loud singing.

Later, as usual, there was the Hallelujah Chorus from the Messiah and we all had to stand. I felt a bit silly, and ma was objecting to being there at all anyway. She doesn't mix with pa's chapel folk if she can help it. Afterwards we walked down the hill to call on Uncle Herbert Preston. He played a record on his gramophone of Herbert Dawson singing 'The Floral Dance'. We played with balloons. Their settee and chairs are all shiny brown leather. Auntie Janey laughed all the time, and Uncle Herbert kept saying what a good service it had been. We went home on the tram to Bingley.

* Methodist Free Church

from *"A Diary of a Bingley Boy,1925–42"*
– an unpublished autobiography
by Herbert Whone.

Holmfirth Parish Church, from Bunkers Hill

The demonstration last Saturday, of the various Nonconformist Sunday Schools of Huddersfield and the immediate neighbourhood, was in every respect thoroughly successful. Twenty thousand Sunday School Scholars and Teachers, walking in procession through the streets, presented the most interesting and heart-moving sight that Huddersfield has hitherto seen or is likely to see. . . . The appearance of Scholars and Teachers was in every way creditable, and the well-dressed and respectable looking children and young people bore the strongest testimony to the beneficial effects of Sunday School training, in its calling forth right influences, and strengthening right principles, in the minds of the young. A community which could send forth, chiefly from the working classes, such a bright, cheerful, orderly multitude, needing no police to restrain or direct it, must be sound at heart, and may justly expect better days in the future than any that have been experienced in the past.

Such armies of the young soldiers of Christ are infinitely more powerful in promoting the safety, the welfare, and the glory of our country, than the armies of fighting men, which cost so much to make them efficient slayers of their fellow-creatures.

Leader in the *"Huddersfield Examiner"*
August 21st, 1880.

188

HUDDERSFIELD CHORAL
SOCIETY

SESSION 1936-1937

The 347 CONCERT
Tuesday Dec. 22 1936
at 7 p.m. in the Town Hall

"MESSIAH"

HANDEL

Principals:

Isobel Baillie
Gladys Ripley
Walter Widdop
Harold Williams

Conductor:

Dr. Malcolm Sargent
F.R.C.M.

Chorus Master:

Herbert Bardgett, Mus.B.,
F.R.C.O.

Leader: Reginald Stead
Solo Trumpet: John Paley
Deputy Chorus Master and
accompanist: Ernest Cooper
F.R.C.O., L.R.A.M.

Honley, Huddersfield

Burnett Street, Bradford

A magpie behold, and a fly and a flea,
And a Yorkshireman's qualifications you'll see,
To backbite and spunge and to chatter amain,
Or anything else sir, by which he can gain.
The horse shows they buy a few tho' many they steal,
Hang'd they're worth nought does the gammon reveal;
But let censure stand by, and not bias the mind,
For others as bad as the Yorkshire you'll find.

from *A Yorkshire Man's Coat of Arms*
an 18th Century proverb
published by O. Hodgson, London

Kirkgate Market, Bradford

King Cross, Halifax

All Square

Pull 'em daan!
Pull 'em daan!
Owd-fashioned buildings.
Slam up some new stuff,
Tall an' four square.
Neer mahnd fowks feelings –
Curves ar' fer weaklings –
Just have 'em bare.

Rahve 'em daan!
Rahve 'em daan!
Aart-o-date buildings;
Ram up some concrete
Set hard an' straight.
Fix some square winders,
Fancy stuff hinders;
Give 'em some height.

Yahke 'em daan!
Yahke 'em daan!
Hed-ther-day buildings;
Square men wi' rulers
Carn't abahde these.

But ther' are consolations,
Wi' all ther square notations –
They carn't grow square trees.

from a collection of poems
The Muse Went Weaving
Fred Brown

Exchange Station, Bradford

"Well, it's been a grand match today, it has," says Mr. Oakroyd dreamily. "I nivver want to see a better. Eh, it were t'owd form all ower again. Them last two goals – nay by gow!"

"Ay, them wor a bit of all right."

"All right! They wor *grand!*"

And then we hear no more. The tide of caps and men flows on, slowly but gradually gathering speed, like our years. It recedes, shrinks, until at last you do not notice it at all. Manchester Road is now only one of a hundred thorough-fares, for Bruddersford itself, the whole spread of it, has come into view. Holdsworth's giant mill looms there on the left; the Midland Railway's station glitters in the sun again, and there is an answering gleam from the glass roof of the Market Hall; a silver stream shows one of the canals, and in the centre of the tall chimneys, shaking the air with its *Lass of Richmond Hill,* is the tower of Bruddersford Town Hall. It points a finger at us, and then is gone, lost in the faint smudge of smoke. Another moment and Bruddersford is only a grimy crack in the hills. The high moorland between Yorkshire and Lancashire rises steadily, clear in the pearly light of Spring. Once more, the miles and miles of ling and bog and black rock, and the curlews crying above the scattered jewellery of the little tarns. There are the Derbyshire hills, and there, away to the north, are the great fells of Cumberland, and now the whole darkening length of it, from the Peak to Cross Fell is visible, for this is the Pennine Range, sometimes called the backbone of England.

from *The Good Companions*
J. B. Priestley (published 1929)

PLACE NAMES TO PHOTOGRAPHS

Glossary of Dialect Words

Page 18–19	*rowt*	worked	*wuther'd*	roared
	maun	mown	*mawl*	mallet
	swealed	melted or wasted	*frame*	prepare
	cannal	candle	*pobs*	porridge
	tew	toil, work hard	*temm'd*	poured
	futtered	bustled		

Page 34	*ass-hoil*	place under the fire where the ashes fall
Page 42	*bahdin'*	biding, waiting
	lig	lie
Page 46	*havercake*	oatcake
	breead-fleck	a rack pulled up by a cord to the ceiling where bread dries out before eating
Page 68–69	*pinder*	keeper of the pinfold for cattle
	duck under	
	water kit	a well known game at festive times – a *kit* is a pail with two handles
	frog-loup	leap-frog
	furinners	foreigner, outsider
Page 81	*mullock and moil*	*mullock* denotes a mess, a blunder, and *moil* denotes drudgery or work
	t'perch	pieces of cloth when finished are placed over a pole or perch to be examined
	capt	astonished
Page 82	*shoo*	she
	nop	head
Page 98	*cuttle*	a method of folding cloth
Page 99	*slay-board*	the board across which the shuttle runs
	camlet	type of cloth for making a camlet, or cloak
Page 110	*guttle*	eat gluttonously

Page 127	*bud*	but	*allus*	always
	flaid	afraid	*meil*	meal
	kal abaht	play about, gossip idly	*mooild*	denotes a
	broil	get heated up		moody temper
	leets	lives		
Page 128	*gloared*	stared hard	*dlow*	glow
	gerse	grass		

Page 132	*brandree*	small iron frame with iron bars and feet put on the fire to rest pans on
Page 148	*thoil*	bear, take it: a word having many subtleties of meaning
Page 151	*spuffle*	fuss, excitement
Page 166	*betterny-bodies*	superior people
	dizen	dress, deck, in an extravagant way
Page 169	*ween*	whin or gorse
Page 173	*o'th'gate*	out of the way
	shives	slices

Biographical Notes

William Cudworth (1830-1906): born at Bradford; began his career in printing and moved later to the editorial staff of the *Yorkshire Observer*. Was one of the founders of the Bradford Historical and Antiquarian Society: devoted his life to studying and writing about local history and archaeology in the Bradford area. Is well known for his book *Round about Bradford,* published 1876.

J. Horsfall Turner (1845–1915); born in Brighouse. Was a social worker especially in the field of temperance. Did antiquarian research and work on non-conformist history, the Brontës and genealogy. Later his work centred around Halifax. Connected with the Yorkshire Dialect Society.

John Hartley (1839–1915): born Halifax. The most well known and prolific of the West Riding dialect writers. Son of a tea merchant, he was himself a designer of worsted goods. In 1867 he founded *The Halifax Illuminated Clock Almanack* and in 1868 published poems under the title *Hartley's Yorkshire Ditties.* From then on, except for two visits to America, he continued to write essays, pamphlets and poems in dialect.

J. Keighley Snowden (1870-1932): born Haworth. Early part of life spent in Bingley where his father was headmaster of Bingley Grammar School. He read mathematics at Cambridge. From the age of 23 he devoted his life to writing. *A Man of the Moors* made him famous. He popularised the dales in *The Striding Dales* and *O'er Moor and Fell,* written in the '20s.

F. W. Moorman (1872–1919): born at Ashburton. Professor of English Language at Leeds University from 1909–19. Connected with the Yorkshire Dialect Society as Editorial Secretary. Among his scholarly books he produced *Tales of the Ridings* and *Songs of the Ridings.*

John Nicholson (1790–1843): born Weardley near Harewood, and became known as the Airedale Poet, because of his interest in Airedale history. Lived at Eldwick, and was a wool-sorter when not selling his poetry. Dissipated life led to death by accident in the River Aire. *Airedale in Ancient Times* made his success as a poet in 1825. (He was not a writer in dialect.)

Ben Preston (1819–1902): born Bradford. His father was a hand-loom weaver. He himself was a woolsorter and began to write in dialect when an apprentice. He bought an allotment and built a house near Shipley Glen, and became known as the Burns of Bradford. His first book of dialect poems was published in 1872.

D. F. Sykes (1856–1920): born and lived in Huddersfield area. Was a brilliant scholar in his youth. Became a solicitor in partnership with his father, and engaged actively in local government. He wrote books about the Huddersfield district and some novels centred around local history.

Ben Turner (1863–1942): born at Holmfirth, Huddersfield. Worked in the mills and brought up in a politically conscious household. Became chairman of the T.U.C. in 1928. A poet, politician, mayor of Batley 1914–16, and knighted in 1931. Wrote in dialect for local papers and published poetry.

William Wright (1836–1897): born in the Hoylus End cottages at Hermit Hole near Keighley, thus the name he used and is known by – Bill o'th'Hoylus End. He was a man of many parts – soldier, sailor, playwright, woolcomber and latter and more consistently warp-dresser. He wrote poetry, pamphlets, and started an Almanack. There is a rustic strength in his work: drink figures frequently, and he was a "character" in his time. He shares with Ben Preston the distinction of being one of the outstanding dialect writers of his age.